ÉMILE ZOLA

# My Reading

RACHEL BOWLBY

# ÉMILE ZOLA

*Writing Modern Life*

**UNIVERSITY PRESS**

Great Clarendon Street, Oxford, OX2 6DP,
United Kingdom

Oxford University Press is a department of the University of Oxford.
It furthers the University's objective of excellence in research, scholarship,
and education by publishing worldwide. Oxford is a registered trade mark of
Oxford University Press in the UK and in certain other countries

© Rachel Bowlby 2025

The moral rights of the author have been asserted

All rights reserved. No part of this publication may be reproduced, stored in a retrieval system, transmitted, used for text and data mining, or used for training artificial intelligence, in any form or by any means, without the prior permission in writing of Oxford University Press, or as expressly permitted by law, by licence or under terms agreed with the appropriate reprographics rights organization. Enquiries concerning reproduction outside the scope of the above should be sent to the Rights Department, Oxford University Press, at the address above

You must not circulate this work in any other form
and you must impose this same condition on any acquirer

Published in the United States of America by Oxford University Press
198 Madison Avenue, New York, NY 10016, United States of America

British Library Cataloguing in Publication Data
Data available
Library of Congress Control Number: 2024946505
ISBN 9780198874126
DOI: 10.1093/oso/9780198874126.001.0001
Printed and bound by
CPI Group (UK) Ltd, Croydon, CR0 4YY

Links to third party websites are provided by Oxford in good faith and
for information only. Oxford disclaims any responsibility for the materials
contained in any third party website referenced in this work.

The manufacturer's authorised representative in the EU for product safety is
Oxford University Press España S.A. of El Parque Empresarial San Fernando de Henares, Avenida
de Castilla, 2 – 28830 Madrid (www.oup.es/en or
product.safety@oup.com). OUP España S.A. also acts as importer into Spain
of products made by the manufacturer.

# SERIES INTRODUCTION

This series is built on a simple presupposition: that it helps to have a book recommended and discussed by someone who cares for it. Books are not purely self-sufficient: they need people and they need to get to what is personal within them.

The people we have been seeking as contributors to *My Reading* are readers who are also writers: novelists and poets; literary critics; outside as well as inside universities; but also thinkers from other disciplines—philosophy, psychology, science, theology, and sociology—beside the literary; and, not least of all, intense readers whose first profession is not writing itself but, for example, medicine, or law, or a non-verbal form of art. Of all of them we have asked: what books or authors feel as though they are deeply *yours*, influencing or challenging your life and work, most deserving of rescue and attention, or demanding of feeling and use?

What is it like to love this book? What is it like to have a thought or idea or doubt or memory, not cold and in the abstract, but live in the very act of reading? What is it like to feel, long after, that this writer is a vital part of your life? We ask our authors to respond to such bold questions by writing not conventionally but personally—whatever 'personal' might mean, whatever form or style it might take, for them as individuals. This does not mean overt confession at the expense of a chosen book or author; but nor should our writers be afraid of making autobiographical connections. What was wanted was whatever made for their own hardest thinking in careful relation to quoted sources and specifics. The work was to go on in the taut and resonant space between these readers and their chosen books. And the interest within that area begins precisely when it is no longer clear how much is coming from the text and how much is coming from its readers—where that distinction is no longer easily tenable because neither is sacrificed to the other. That would show what reading meant at its most serious and how it might have a relation to an individual life.

Out of what we hope will be an ongoing variety of books and readers, *My Reading* offers personal models of what it is like to care about particular authors, to recreate through specific examples imaginative versions of what those authors and works represent, and to show their effect upon a reader's own thinking and development.

ANNE CHENG
PHILIP DAVIS
JACQUELINE NORTON
MARINA WARNER
MICHAEL WOOD

# PREFACE

Does anyone still read Zola? As both a real and a rhetorical question (as if we all know the answer), this bemused concern has been a standard starting point for discussions of the novelist in English since at least the middle of the twentieth century. On the one hand, there is an invitation—come on, Zola is a great writer, you should read him. And on the other there is the acknowledgement of some problem: there are reasons, right or wrong, why in fact no one does. Zola is a writer worth reading, it is implied, or a writer we shouldn't not read. But for this or that reason, it seems that we don't very much—at least not in English. Depending on the context, those reasons may be presented as based on a prejudice—a mistake that needs correcting—or else as having to do with something that's really wrong with Zola's novels, and needs to be dealt with so as to then begin the work or the pleasure of reading him at last. It is as if Zola is always in need of the right recommendation, the preliminary defence, against the backdrop of general disregard, or at least of an already settled demotion to second-rate status.

A nice example of this phenomenon occurs in a review from 1953 by the American critic Lionel Trilling of a new book about Zola by the English novelist Angus Wilson. The review is entitled 'In Defense of Zola'. Trilling is appraising Wilson's own strategy in dealing with the general problem of Zola not being read, and proposes his own response:

## PREFACE

> Of the great reputations of the nineteenth century, perhaps none has suffered so much diminution as that of Zola. We all believe that we know all about Zola, whether we have read him or not—we know what he did, and what he stood for, whom he influenced and what his theory of the novel was, and what was wrong with it. But he has not for many years commanded our real interest, precisely, I suppose, because we all believe we have him so thoroughly taped.[1]

This well-informed and unanimous 'we'—'We all believe that we know all about ...'—may seem a far cry from the equivalent twenty-first-century reader or non-reader of Zola, who would probably not be credited with any knowledge, however vague, of Zola's life and work—let alone of his 'theory'. For Trilling, then, Zola's problem is that everyone thinks they know what's wrong with him and therefore why they don't have to bother with reading him.

Angus Wilson, in the book that Trilling is reviewing, had stated the case for Zola's (regrettable) neglect from a different angle. Not long ago, he implies, nineteenth-century novelists were generally ignored. Now they are not—but Zola has somehow missed out:

> There has, in the last twenty years, been a rehabilitation or, at any rate, a serious defence of most of the nineteenth-century novelists, whose pretensions—in their own day—were to the highest rank. Zola, however, has continued to lie neglected in the dusty cupboard to which he had already been consigned by many younger French writers in his own lifetime.[2]

He has been stuck in an attic for decades. The problem has been, in part, those 'embarrassingly naïve theories'[3] of his to which Trilling alludes in his review, and also the charge of too much sex, or sex of the wrong kind: 'Zola has been declared not only obscene, but childishly so, and worse still, old-fashioned in his obscenity. To read his work seriously has been like facing the imputation of telling an old dirty joke.'[4] Once, people did take Zola seriously, and seriously read his work; now, they don't, and so it is time to show why it is important to read him. The writer of the critical book is on a modest mission: 'If the present small work does no more than encourage a few readers to unlock the rusty cupboard which contains so much delight, it will have served its purpose.'[5] Dusty or rusty, an opening up of the closet is overdue; in it is no skeleton but a vital and enjoyable body of work.

Quite a few readers clearly did take an interest in the key that Wilson offered, even if they may not have got to the point of using it. His book had a second edition in the mid-1960s, as did another engagingly readable critical monograph about Zola by the Leicester academic F.W.J. Hemmings, which had come out shortly after Wilson's.[6] In 1969, for a special issue of the journal *Yale French Studies*, the critic Naomi Schor is able to refer to an ongoing 'revival' of interest in Zola's work, while the preface to the second edition of Hemmings's book, a few years before, speaks expansively: 'Since this book was written, in 1951-2, more work has been done on Zola than over the whole of the previous period since his death in 1902.'[7]

That critical enterprise has continued in all the subsequent decades, in French primarily, with the publication of scholarly editions of many kinds of accessory materials, from the complete correspondence to the extensive preparatory dossiers that Zola compiled for each one of his many novels. But still there remains, when it comes to the question of reading the novels themselves, a suggestion of Wilson's abandoned old volumes stored away. It is as if Zola is always taken to have been cast out of the main room of critical approval or celebration; and that therefore it must be the job of a new critic coming along to acknowledge that predicament and then, in the light of their own curiosities, to seek out the key to the Zola cupboard for anyone else who would care to enjoy its contents.

Sometimes the rhetoric of reappraisal involves a persona other than that of the settled Zola advocate who seeks to enlighten further readers; instead, as though against their own better judgement, the writer proclaims the unexpected pleasures to be found in reading Zola. In a review by Michael Wood in 2014 of a book by Fredric Jameson, the critic emerges from a state of initial prejudice into the newfound light of Zola-appreciation: 'Jameson finds affect in the profusion of Zola's France, the streets, the shops, the light, the crowds, the objects and animals, and his amazing examples—dead fish in a market, an array of cheeses, an ocean of white cloths in a department store—made me feel that Zola was a great writer I hadn't even started to read.'[8] The implication is that unlike Flaubert, say, another focus of Jameson's book and Wood's review of it, Zola had not until now been granted the prior acceptance of being that kind of writer you would naturally read with seriousness and attention (and who you would be embarrassed not to have read); that the block was there, or the door was locked, was itself something taken for granted.

The trio of passages Wood admires from Jameson's long quotations have something in common, which is that they all describe displays of goods for sale: two in the Paris food market, Les Halles, which is the setting of *Le Ventre de Paris* (*The Belly of Paris*)

(1873), and the other (the display of fabrics he mentions) from *Au Bonheur des Dames* (*The Ladies' Paradise*) (1883), whose title is the name of the Paris department store where it is set. Zola has an eye for the aesthetic potency of shops and market stalls, which draw on the senses of touch and smell as well as the visual *éclat* of the massing and juxtaposition of colours. There is an appeal and a beauty in these everyday works of art. Repeatedly, Zola praises the aesthetic gifts of Octave Mouret, the director of the department store, even as he displays his own talent for the verbal evocation of this merchandising magic. His listings of all the glorious and gorgeous names of edible cheeses and touchable stuffs graft together the commercial and the epic, whereby Homer's majestic mustering in the 'catalogue of the ships' in Book II of the *Iliad* joins forces with a modern showcasing of every splendid commodity that money can buy. These passages are like brilliant advertisements for all the beautiful things you can see in the market and in the store.

Extended descriptive pieces like the symphony of the cheeses, *la symphonie des fromages* (as it is lovingly known to connoisseurs), stand out in Zola's work; it is not by chance that Jameson quotes them at such length, or that they appear to suspend their novel's story with the sheer pleasure of dwelling here, in this passage and in this place, with all its attendant colours and smells and sounds. Like the novel itself they are put together by the imaginative work of a skilled creative hand: the market trader or (in Octave Mouret's case) the owner of the department store. Zola's novels abound in illustrations of such everyday aesthetics, which are like analogues of the writer's own practice in his presentation. Across all his novels, he opens up spaces and sections of ordinary life, cupboards whose contents have never before been the object

PREFACE

of literary appraisal—and never before been seen by or shown to readers.

In keeping with the ethos of the *My Reading* series—and with the long history of Zola promotions—this book is meant as a kind of extended advertisement for Zola: that is, I want to communicate my own Zola enthusiasms, and thus to persuade readers to want to read Zola too. The book is not written for specialists, and does not assume any knowledge of French. I have tried to make it readable, meaning clear and interesting. Zola, who wrote with extraordinary lucidity, was always, somehow, both.

Zola's writing has always been primarily associated with the presentation or exposure of lower-class working life—above all in his best-selling novels of all time, *L'Assommoir* (1877) and *Germinal* (1880). The first of these is about precarious lives in Paris, the second about a mining district in the north of France. These were novels that created new literary territory. But he also wrote about many other settings, from a bourgeois apartment building (*Pot-Bouille*) to small-town politics (*La Fortune des Rougon*) to life on the railways (*La Bête humaine*) to wartime life for both soldiers and civilians (*La Débâcle*). There is a novel about the banking world (*L'Argent*) and another about a provincial priest (*La Faute de l'abbé Mouret*). And there is so much more. Much, if not all, of mid- to late nineteenth-century French human life is there—testimony to the extraordinary documentary scope and skill of this new kind of writer-journalist.

In the space of a short book, I can only begin to give a sense of all that is to be found in Zola's writings. Rather than going through novel by novel—too many by far!—or selecting a small number for extended individual readings, I have followed a simple three-part division which is designed to illustrate some of the ways Zola wrote, and some of the unlikely sides and corners of modern life that he noticed and put into prose. The first chapter, 'Introductions', is about how Zola represents types and characters. Then 'Milieux', in the middle, looks at Zola's attention to specific environments in setting the terms for likely behaviours and events. 'Endings', finally, is about plots, and the many kinds of story at play in the last decade of Zola's life.

Chapter 1 introduces Zola's work by way of his character types and by looking, one-sidedly, at the curious case of the *profile*. This is a word that often crops up in relation to the first appearance of a new character in a novel, and which is suggestive of issues that surround the representation of persons both in fiction and in real life. A profile is normally an outline or summary, a first impression of a type of person; it can also suggest a hidden or ominous other aspect, not seen in what is overtly just a side view. This chapter takes its examples mainly from Zola's earlier work and is also, more broadly, a profile of some of the features of his writing.

The second chapter, 'Milieux', looks at Zola's socially spot-on settings. Fundamental to the Rougon-Macquart novels of his middle years, these milieux were anything but incidental backgrounds, subordinate to the story or the style. Before the plotting or the writing itself, they were the object of detailed research—through reading, and also on location, in the places and workplaces that were to feature in the novel. For Zola, the milieu determined the way that characters might think and behave, and the kinds of plot or story that might play out between them. As exemplary milieux I focus on Zola's shops, in part because a shop is by definition a 'middle' or intermediate place, where goods are swapped for money on their way from production to consumption, but also because for me these many and multifarious Zolian outlets have been the beginning and middle and ongoing discoveries in my own appreciation of Zola's work.

The third chapter, 'Endings', turns to plots and *dénouements*—in novels and in reality. Public and personal stories of many kinds clash and combine in Zola's last years. In the late 1890s he became one of the protagonists of the protracted campaign to exonerate Alfred Dreyfus, the Jewish army officer falsely accused of treason. In the course of that process Zola spent almost a year of exile in England, away from his wife, Alexandrine, and also from his two young children and their mother, Jeanne Rozerot. During this time he wrote a novel, *Fécondité*, a passionate contribution to contemporary arguments about the politics of reproduction—and he also wrote letters, constantly, which are a fruitful source for thinking about the relationships between daily and longer-term narratives and histories. The last sections of this chapter, finally, look at some stories and theories that bear on our understanding of Zola's sudden death in the autumn of 1902.

# CONTENTS

*A Note on Texts and Translations*     xvii

1. Introductions: Characters: Profiles     1
   - Invitation to tea     1
   - Profile of the profile     4
   - Social types     7
   - The view of the city     14
   - Historical profiles     18
   - Experimenting with novels     22
   - Sex in the shadows     28
   - Social problems     32
   - Sexual observations     36
   - Roles     44

2. Milieux: In the Middle: Shops     47
   - Shopping milieux     47
   - Within the arcade     55
   - In the big store     60
   - Sexual pressures     64
   - Local ambitions     68
   - Modern retail style     77

3. Endings: Plots: Exile in England     83
   - The Dreyfus affair and beyond     83
   - Working, living     87
   - The consolations of daily life     93
   - Antenatal, anti-anti-natal: *Fécondité*     100
   - Afterstories     115
   - 'Fire!'     125

## CONTENTS

*Notes* 135
*Acknowledgements* 149
*Bibliography* 150
*Index* 155

# A NOTE ON TEXTS AND TRANSLATIONS

All unattributed translations of Zola and other writers are my own.

Where published translations of Zola's novels are available, page references are given to English as well as French texts, for ease of reference. These translations are frequently modified—'tr. mod.'— in the citations: not to correct them, but to bring out particular aspects of a passage in line with the ongoing discussion.

Titles of Zola's novels are given in French, with an English version, if different, in brackets at the first mention in each chapter. Original French titles are needed because in many cases there is more than one English title in different published translations of the same book. *Pot-Bouille*, for instance, which means ordinary home cooking, has appeared in English as *Piping Hot*, or *Pot Roast*, as well as just the raw (unmodified) *Pot-Bouille*. *La Bête humaine*, equally metaphorical, is *The Beast Within* or *The Beast in Man*—or else simply *La Bête humaine*. For default, I have used the titles (and translations) of the Oxford World's Classics series. Where a novel's title is a name, or otherwise identical (or nearly) in its translated version, it is not repeated before a page reference in English.

# 1

# INTRODUCTIONS CHARACTERS PROFILES

### Invitation to tea

Let us begin with a gathering of society ladies in a drawing room. In an early episode of *Au Bonheur des Dames* (*The Ladies' Paradise*) (1883), Zola's novel about the life of a department store, a group of ladies are taking tea at the home of their wealthy friend, the widowed Henriette Desforges. Also of the party is Octave Mouret, the ambitious owner of the store. Mme Desforges is his mistress, and Mouret has come along mostly for the chance of being introduced to another male guest, Baron Hartmann—modelled on Baron Haussmann, the maestro of Paris's mid-century building transformation. Mouret is hoping the Baron can be induced to become an investor in his plans to expand his store into the neighbouring streets.

That is the masculine side of the occasion. The women guests, meanwhile, are all customers at the store as well as friends of their hostess. They are delighted to have the chance of talking to Mouret, revered as the glamorous initiator of their newfound shopping enjoyments. One of them, Mme Marty, has even come straight from the store, with her typically too many purchases, at first secreted in her handbag and then passed round for the others to gasp at admiringly.

Over a slow unfolding of several pages, Zola shows us around the several separate little dramas going on—from a tense interaction between Octave and Henriette to the separation of masculine and feminine conversations after the Baron arrives and the two men are taken through to another room so that Mouret can make his pitch. A couple of other men arrive: the husband of one of the women, accompanied by their daughter's fiancé, M. Vallagnosc. Extracts of talk are deftly interspersed with descriptions of the décor in the apartment, and back-story information such as Henriette's prior relationship with the much older Baron and his readiness, in an avuncular way, to do her the favour of supporting his younger successors. The polite passing of the afternoon is punctuated now and then by brief passages calling attention to the gradual decline of the light outside the windows; these passages are like the familiar, repeated lines of long epic poems like the *Odyssey* or *Iliad*, anchoring the action to the time of day.

At the very end of the scene, and the day, Zola brings into focus the star player for the assembled audience, and also introduces one last new character. Octave Mouret has just been led back into the room where the women are waiting to grab him; during his absence they have been talking of nothing else but the bargains, present and future, on offer at the store:

> A hubbub of triumph greeted him. He had to come forward further, the women made room for him in the middle of them. The sun had just set behind the trees in the garden, the day was

declining, a delicate shadow was gradually engulfing the vast room. It was the gentle time of dusk, that minute of discreet pleasure in Paris apartments, between the light of the dying street and the lamps that are still being lit inside. M. de Boves and M. Vallagnosc, still standing in front of the window, cast a pool of shadow onto the carpet. Motionless, meanwhile, in the last beam of light coming from the other window, M. Marty, who had come in unobtrusively a few minutes before, added his impoverished profile [*profil pauvre*], his skimpy, clean frock-coat, his face faded from his teaching job; he was now in the process of being thoroughly upset by these women's talk about clothes.[1]

Mouret occupies the central position, celebrated and on the rise; he is the star and the sun of this bright little world as the real sun declines on the horizon. M. Marty, creeping in, is obscure. His income is low and his wife is the over-spender of the group; he has slipped in unnoticed by the women and also by the narrative, up to this point. Zola slides him into the background, just as the light is falling and this unique occasion today in Henriette's drawing room drifts out into the typicality of a daily occurrence in every apartment in Paris. It is like a snapshot, 'that minute', this one time, but it is also generic and vague in its fading of light into dark: the poetic *crépuscule* of a Paris dusk. A pathetic figure—and only a figure, an outline—M. Marty comes into the paragraph as the third additional man, after the already shadowy pair of M. de Boves and his companion. His *profil pauvre*, his poor little profile, is as if reduced or worn down, like his clothes and his hardworking life.

M. Marty has come late; he is only just picking up on what is being said and, though this is not stated directly, on its implications for himself as a provider of limited means whose household, sure enough, will provide the novel's exemplary story of how a store like Au Bonheur des Dames can cause ruinous debt. But if M. Marty is only half informed, a partial interpreter of what he is hearing the end of, then so, from the reader's point of view, are we. This limited vision—the character's and the reader's—is exactly captured by the indication of the 'profile'—*profil*—the term used here by Zola.

## Profile of the profile

The profile, in this instance, is an introduction, a preliminary and partial view which may or may not be amplified with the provision of a fuller picture. By definition, a profile is a side view; it is one side only, with another side that is not visible. This partial aspect lends the profile two different kinds of likely suggestion when the word appears in a piece of descriptive prose. It may simply imply that we don't know much about the individual in profile beyond the outline of some external or general features. It may also point to an actively hidden dimension, whether inviting or disturbing. When the profile is also, as it is here, associated with an absence of light, the shadowy appearance will compound the possible sense of mystery or menace. In this instance M. Marty is harmless in himself; but he is not really part of this gathering. If he is only a shadowy presence, it is not that he is a threat, but that he is out of place. His situation undermines the excitement engendered by Mouret's triumphant presence.

Making its first appearance in the eighteenth century as a term of art criticism, the word 'profile' specifically designated a side-on head-and-shoulders portrait. The word has undergone a long and varied history since its beginnings, alongside the silhouette, as a new style of portraiture, but it remains rooted in this visual and aesthetic origin. Often understood almost interchangeably, the silhouette and the profile both depend on an outline and on a contrast of light and dark. As such, they are as if natural candidates for the suggestion of an equivocal view or description: a person seen in profile is only half seen.

There is a longer history to the suggestiveness of the profile aspect before the word itself was commonly used. The theologian Rowan Williams, in a lecture of 2019, describes 'the extreme rarity of any depiction of anyone in profile' in religious icons. He goes on:

> Profile means a lack of communion or communication. The figure depicted in profile in the icon is not relating either to God or the beholder and is therefore someone you ought to look at rather suspiciously. You will have endless examples of three-quarter portrayals, but strict *profiles* are rare. Demons appear to profile because they have the strongest vested interest in preventing communion with anybody at all. And you will sometimes see what you might call 'neutral' figures depicted in profile—by which I mean figures who don't have a very marked role in the story. In the icon of the nativity, you will quite often see a stray shepherd chatting to Joseph in the corner, and this figure is quite regularly shown in profile, not because he is diabolical but simply because he doesn't actually matter a great deal in this event.[2]

Already here there is the double possibility of the profile: either mysterious and quite likely evil or else neutrally secondary: a person of relative unimportance within the narrative. Zola himself, in the second part of his *Lettre à la jeunesse* (1879), has a devil in profile. He is referring to the image given to the scholar Ernest Renan after the publication of his humanizing—and therefore, to many, blasphemous—*Vie de Jésus* (*The Life of Jesus*), in 1863: 'M. Renan was unknown to the public ... And suddenly, in the space of a day, his face rose up over France, with the terrifying profile of the Antichrist.'[3]

The profile also has many modern developments—which need no introduction. More verbal than visual now, more digital than descriptive, we all have them—lots and lots of them. We make them, we deal with them all the time in the online domains of our lives, across all shades of social media and everyday sign-up ('Thank you for updating your profile!'). In its modern sense the profile provides a certain amount of information according to an agreed set of classifications for a given and specifiable situation—from online dating to customer loyalty schemes. Already in Zola's time the profile could have this typological sense, which is fundamental to his own way of seeing the world and writing about it. Like Balzac before him, he frequently uses the casually classifying formula 'one of those ...', *un de ces*—as in 'one of those women who rarely bought anything', or 'the kind of person who likes to take their time'. This is the everyday profiling of real life and realist literature. It marks out a trait or behavioural habit that is distinctive but also recognizable, nameable, and shared with others: something that is not unique to this person but observable as a familiar type within the culture. The nineteenth century invented it and needed it, in keeping with the proliferation of all sorts of roles and ways of being in the different sections of modern society.

If seen in half light, in a shadowy place, the profile is not black and white, yet it depends on the colourless contrast that makes or marks an outline. There is a comparable dual aspect to the modern social profile. It may be potentially damning, as in the sketching of the likely appearance of an as yet unidentified criminal, or in the casual, everyday profiling which casts those with certain characteristics as more or less likely to act in certain ways. Or else it may be more upbeat, as in the invitation to complete if not create your 'own' profile—a profile that, for all its supposed individuality, will also be specifying the person according to established terms of classification ('Would you describe yourself as …?'). This composition of personal profiles, so called, for platforms designed to present yourself in the best light for the role of a prospective employee or partner—for instance—is one of the new skills or arts of the online twenty-first century. Show your best side.

## Social types

In *Aspects of the Novel*, in 1928, the English novelist E.M. Forster divided the population of fictional works into flat and round characters.[4] The round characters are the whole people, fully developed from all points of view in the course of a given novel. Flat characters are the ones described with no more than a quick summing up, as if known in advance or as if there is not a lot to be said about them. As with a profile, 'flat' characters are (literally, in the word) two-dimensional.

Forster's account was practical; for the sake of artistic coherence, a novel has to focus on a few of its characters only. He did not mean to divide the real world of human beings into the two categories of those endowed with a comprehensive personhood and those who have to make do with the minimal version, who fall short of fullness. But the division has often been treated as if that had been his meaning. Or, in the same vein, it has been taken up as a way of objecting to the simplified characterization of this or that character in a given novel, with the implication that they have been deprived of the authorial attention that any character, like any human being, has a right to deserve. In this way, the formal dissection of a novel's conditions of existence—it is bound to concentrate on some people, if not some one person, more than others—soon crosses into political and ethical territory. Why did the author choose to focus on this kind of person, not that? The queen as opposed to the cook? The lawyer—white and male and French-born and middle-aged, though all of those qualities go without saying—rather than the taxi driver, different in all but one of those features, who picks him up at the station? In this way, the politics of representation directly enters into the micro-worlds of the novel.

Zola's encyclopaedic collection of characters and milieux in the many novels of the Rougon-Macquart series does not discriminate by class or region or sex. He concentrates in different contexts on different characters—or, conversely, at different times he will relegate a given category of person to the second-order status of Forster's flat characters. This is not to say that his portrayals of everyone in every kind of social position are always commensurate with twenty-first-century expectations or norms (which vary, in any case, from one reader—and one milieu—to another). How could they be? On the other hand, he will sometimes shift the perspective so that a character who until now has occupied a minor place is suddenly brought into the centre. By the end of *La Joie de vivre* (*The Bright Side of Life*) (1884), readers are familiar with the bleak existence of the family living on the Normandy coast whose collective life, over many years, has been a succession of crises and failures; the irony of the novel's upbeat name is part of its atmosphere of perpetual negativity, which includes the period's signature sign of cultural despair, a Schopenhauer-reading youth. Then at the end, without any explanation on her part or anyone else's, the family's long-term live-in servant Véronique suddenly hangs herself from a pear tree in the garden. In the same way as the novel's readers, the family are confronted with the fact that this woman who has been keeping everyone going from day to day with her advice of all kinds, as well as her cooking and cleaning, is unknown to them as a person. 'But why?' exclaimed Pauline. 'She had no reason; she'd even started making dinner.'[5] It is a commentary—all the more effective for being unelaborated—on the neglect of a servant by her employers, within her own world; she is there in their midst but she has been unregarded—a depthless, flat character—for all those around her.

Paradoxically, then, the characters singled out for a rounded treatment, in Forster's terms, are normally those who in social terms need no introduction because their dominant markers—of class, sex, and race—are taken for granted. The other side of this situation is the reduction of other types—of half the human population, say—to the flat status of being as if known in advance: she is like this because that's the way women are. A 'stereotype' is literally a hard imprint, fixing one version of people according to some characteristic that has been taken to determine what—or 'who'—they are.

Would-be writers of fiction today are often urged to write about 'what you know'—that is, from direct familiarity with the kind of social world or life experience to be shown. The suggestion is, on the one hand, that you are better qualified to write about these things precisely because you have been there and been involved; you have not been a detached observer, viewing abstractly or at a distance. And on the other hand, that if you are not familiar with a given milieu or experience, then it is not for you to write about since you lack that qualification or entitlement. The implicit requirement of a degree of authorial involvement consciously steps away from the now discredited set-up, characterized as that of the 'omniscient' narrator of the nineteenth-century realist novel. This divinely all-knowing personage assumes a position from which they neutrally observe and report on the movements and motives of the characters of their fictional creation. The narrator knows everything about everyone but they are supposedly themselves without distinguishing features of any kind—not even the gender of 'he' or 'she', one or the other, that is grammatically indispensable to most forms of human worldly existence. In a novel, no character refers to the narrator narrating them; that narrator remains as if out of the fray, sublimely neutral.

In reality—the reality of existing novels, as opposed to the theory of them—few narratives and narrators, even those from the peak nineteenth-century time of a now maligned realist literature, did assume that as if all-encompassing perspective from which their chosen bit of the world might be neutrally surveyed and described. Zola's position is other than this, in any case. It is not that he puts himself in the picture by any direct acknowledgement of a founding or central narrative role; he doesn't, for instance, like Thackeray or Trollope, adopt a persona and take the reader aside for a chat about what is going on in the novel. Instead, his situations and characters derive from knowledge that has been methodically acquired by a pre-novel process of real-world research. In the case of *Au Bonheur des Dames*, he spent time at two existing department stores—the Bon Marché and the Louvre—learning about the marketing theories that were—as he puts it in the novel—'revolutionizing' modern retail practice. He interviewed those involved in every aspect of the business and took copious notes which then became the basis for the elaboration of representative characters and scenarios. Essentially, this was immersive reportage with the storylines having the function of case studies in long-form journalism, or a piece of sociological research. In this sense, different from the experiential expectation of contemporary creative writing, Zola did write about what he knew.

All the women guests in Zola's teatime scene are flat characters in Forster's sense; their narrative purpose is to constitute a spectrum of typical shopping behaviours, which Zola will then utilize in the rest of the novel with all the profiling precision of a modern market researcher. In Henriette's drawing room they are each captured in a summarizing paragraph which catalogues them one by one:

> And beneath the chattering curiosity with which they assailed the young man, there appeared their individual buying personalities: Mme Marty, carried away by her spending craze, taking everything at the Bonheur des Dames, without making a selection, whatever was on display; Mme Guibal, walking around there for hours without ever making a purchase, happy and satisfied just with a feast for her eyes; Mme de Boves, on a tight budget, always tortured by too much wanting, resentful towards the merchandise, that she couldn't take away with her; Mme Bourdelais, with her sensible, practical middle-class flair, going straight for the sales goods. With her consummate housewifely skills, not getting over-excited, she made such good use of the department stores that she managed to make substantial savings there.[6]

The capsule descriptions programmatically provide a reading guide for the comments each woman is making in the ongoing teatime conversation. Each of these individual attitudes will then be played out in later scenes taking place in the store itself; each represents a possible response to the framing environment which is this new kind of retail establishment and its new way of selling its wares.

In all his novels, Zola's practice is to introduce recurring but intermittent characters with the same turns of phrase, like a capsule summary or reminder to the reader of who this is. Zola has always been known—and criticized—for his repetitions, sometimes amounting to several sentences at a go; one context for that criticism, as Andrew Counter has argued, is the default condemnation of such habits as lazy and lacking in style. But as Counter convincingly suggests, in Zola's case there need be no contradiction between 'the "readable" and the "innovative"'.[7] Again, the comparison with Homeric epic is useful: for a long production, such as an oral poem, or, in Zola's time, a very long novel serialized in a newspaper, the characters come bearing the same epithets or miniature profiles each time they appear, like an extension of their name. These set-piece outlines may also, as with the various types of shopper, reinforce an informative function. They illustrate likely modes of behaviour in relation to the particular milieu with which the novel is concerned.

In *Âu Bonheur des Dames* the distribution of consumerly orientations among different exemplary female characters is like a detailed enactment of the governing masculine project. This is laid bare on the same tea-party occasion, in a private conversation between the two leading men. Zola flags this up as such, in all its conspiratorial separation from the women in the adjoining room—and thus from all the women who are the explicit targets of commercial manipulation:

> In a few sentences spoken into Baron Hartmann's ear, as if he had been making one of those confessions that are sometimes hazarded between men, he managed to explain the mechanism of large-scale modern retail. Then, higher up than the facts already given, at the very top, there appeared the exploitation of women.[8]

'One of those' again: this is the way men behave, between themselves. The reader too is now initiated into such masculine confidences, both the fact that they happen, generically, and this one in particular. Now, the schematic presentation of female customer types is shown as being not so much a simplification as a demonstration of the spectrum of likely responses to the 'exploitation' of which they are all, collectively, the object. So the reader—woman or man—is given access to the raw reality of what (some) men talk about among themselves and what they knowingly do to women. That is a striking gesture in itself. But Zola's exposure gains further force from its beautifully orchestrated staging in the form of the real separation, on this occasion, between the men and the women, whose own conversation, even away from the store itself, is about nothing else. There is also the detail of Henriette's own situation. She is a wealthy and influential woman, a widow with her own fortune. But here she is doing a feminine favour to both of these powerful men; the alliance between the two of them—including the masculine bonding via intimate talk about women—is allowed to take precedence over her own relationship to each of them.

Apart from such exhibitions of how some men plot out and plan the future directions of their worlds, Zola also explores a more trivial and innocent kind of everyday story-making. Elsewhere in *Au Bonheur des Dames*, for instance, one minor character only features as she is glimpsed, occasionally, by the staff at the store. This is a woman who shows up from time to time on a day trip from 'her province', taking advantage of the cheaper prices in the Paris emporium. She is seen by the novel as briefly and partially as she is seen by the assistants who serve her, who wonder—for something to wonder about—who exactly she might be, or what her story is. Fleetingly coming and going, at regular intervals, a woman like this has the role of an enigmatic character not just for readers but also for the characters within the novel. Daily life is enlivened by the diversion of a small, innocuous mystery and the invention of likely stories in response. On one occasion, for instance, this unknown lady turns up in mourning clothes. Has she lost a husband? Some other family member? The modern urban setting, constantly moving people in and out of its spaces, casts everyone as potentially a figure of minor mystery or possibility, momentarily profiled for others—just as everyone, by the same token, is also given the role of a curious observer of the enigma of other people, all with real lives of their own, all known only by whatever glimpse they may offer or show: their visible profile, open to speculation.

## The view of the city

Such details of local habit and tiny story are at the opposite extreme, the other end of the line, from the grand narrative overview, as if from on high. It is Zola's great gift to be able to do both those things, to hold together different points and angles of view, their contrasting scale and focus: from noting in passing—as she passes—a figure who will play no other part in a novel to pointing towards the bigger picture within which she is situated. This variation of view, from the incidental and local to the widest survey, is fundamental to his understanding of the world he unfolds, piece by piece, in all its corners and complexities.

In western Europe, the nineteenth century was a period of unprecedented social movement, seen and noted as such—with rapidly increasing populations and many more people living in towns and cities as a result of industrialization. There was also the beginning of a general consciousness that the situation of perpetual change was not an aberration from a normal state of relative fixity, but instead the reality of both human and natural life. Evolution was the word that captured that theory; Darwin's *On the Origin of Species* (1859) can be seen as the biological equivalent of the social situation of perpetual tiny changes that Baudelaire, in *Le Peintre de la vie moderne* (*The Painter of Modern Life*) (1863), picked out in the form of daily life and the ever-moving sights and fashions of the city. There was always something new—something new to be curiously noticed, or, in the scientist's terms, *observed*.

Not only was the world now seen as essentially, not occasionally unsettled—always in the process of changing, with no fixed direction—but it was also now more complex and diverse than before. Beyond the now simple-seeming divisions of old social hierarchies and established ways of life, with a broad and simple separation between social classes or between the capital city and the provinces, there was a proliferation of micro-worlds, according to different occupations or industries, all with their own protocols of behaviour and their own specializations of skill and vocabulary, tied to that one small world. There are many possible kinds of situation or origin, each with its own norms of behaviour and identity, and its own internal divisions and conflicts.

In this larger context of change and complexity, Zola took up the task, which was formulated as such, of producing a multi-novel representation of modern French society via what he called the 'natural and social history' of one extended family, the Rougon-Macquarts. In their various capacities and characters and regions, the members of this family would be tracked through the period known as the Second Empire, the 1850s and 1860s. The historical culmination is the Franco-Prussian War of 1870 and the short-lived government of the socialist Commune in Paris that followed it; these events are the subject of *La Débâcle* (1892), the penultimate novel in the series, which ran to twenty novels all told. This was the extraordinary scope of the project: as a study of history so recent as barely to count as history at all: of the just past past, or yesterday's present. But the work was not presented as a chronological sequence, year by year, tracing political developments, or focused on the life of some single character. What Zola did instead was to build up a sense of the diverse social life of those times by looking at multiple separate compartments, or milieux, within it. Thus *Germinal* takes place in a mining community of north-west France. *Pot-Bouille*, meanwhile, is set in an affluent apartment block in Paris. *Le Ventre de Paris* (*The Belly of Paris*) is about the life surrounding Les Halles, the great food market in Paris. In a completely different corner of the Paris economy, *L'Argent* (*Money*) is about the world of banking and speculation, while *La Curée* examines the corrupt machinations of one individual entrepreneur. Several novels, including the first of the series, *La Fortune des Rougon* (*The Fortune of the*

INTRODUCTIONS: CHARACTERS: PROFILES

*Rougons*), look at local politics in a small town in the south of the country—like Aix-en-Provence, where Zola had mainly grown up. *La Bête humaine* takes place on the railways, on one particular line in the north. Along with *Au Bonheur des Dames*, which shows the workings of a department store, this novel looks behind the scenes at a new nineteenth-century industry that, in a short space of time, had radically changed the layout of people's lives.

But the larer picture is always present too as a frame for the separate social arenas in which each of Zola's novels is located. Often the double focus is realized in the form of a directly visual contrast. *Paris* (1898) is one of the long, late novels that followed the completion of the Rougon-Macquart cycle; it is the last of a trilogy set in specific towns or cities (the first two are *Rome* and *Lourdes*). Towards the end of this novel there is a scene in which one of the characters, a sculptor, is looking out from the window of his workshop high up in Montmartre, as evening falls: 'you could see the narrow profiles [*fins profils*] of Antoine, very tall, and of Lise, small and frail, detached against the immensity of Paris, gilded in the sun's farewell'.[9] Here the profiles are small patches of familiarity, coming home; Antoine carries and shelters Lise, the girl he has rehabilitated from a state of physical and mental helplessness. That immensity and grandeur of a Paris beyond the grasp of its individual watchers or walkers is set against the particularity of the pair of awaited loved ones who are on their way home and who can be seen and known; they will be safely back before it is completely dark. Another Paris novel, *Une page d'amour* (*A Love Story*) (1878), returns repeatedly to the view of the city as seen from the apartment of its main character, Hélène, the young widow whose frail little daughter dies in the course of the novel and whose individual story of loving and suffering is counterposed to the vastness of the big city beyond her window and her small locality.

That vastness of the view of Paris from the window of one person's dwelling suggests something beyond the grasp of human perception. Looking out beyond the small compass of that one room, the spectator is diminished and rendered insignificant, in the light and the lights of the sight that surpasses them. Such a situation looks onwards to many twentieth-century vistas, in film most of all, of the vast city all around, as seen in the view from a high-rise apartment block in Manhattan or Tokyo, say. It can also suggest the sheer excitement and opportunity of the multiple personal worlds out there, each with their separate and specific realities. This is how Zola imagines that possibility, for the art of the present, in a newspaper article of 1871:

> I have left my fireplace and, opening the window, I looked out at my beloved, my vast Paris, rushing around in the grey embers of dusk. It is Paris that speaks to me of the new art, with its animated streets, its horizons stained with banners and posters, its houses dreadful and delightful, where there is love and where there is death. Its immense drama is what attaches me to the modern drama, to the existences of its bourgeois and its workers, to all its drifting crowd, whose every pain and every joy I would like to note down.[10]

## Historical profiles

The beginning of *Germinal* (1885) offers another example of the visual contrast of the individual profile with an immense expanse of space, in this case unpeopled. It is the image of one man making his way across a deserted space at night: 'Crossing

## INTRODUCTIONS: CHARACTERS: PROFILES

the open plain, wading through the thick, dark ink of a starless night, a solitary figure followed the highway from Marchiennes to Montsou, which cut its paved pathway straight through ten kilometres of beet fields.'[11] In the darkness he can barely see; there is nothing in front of him but the road; he is hoping that he will be able to warm himself up at one of the pithead braziers that he now perceives, but beyond that immediate ambition, his mind is a blank. He has the 'empty head of a worker without a job and without a home'; the phrasing makes 'jobless and homeless', 'sans travail et sans gîte', a typical situation.[12] These first paragraphs move between the distanced view of the plain and the consciousness of the man as he makes his way forward, until at length he is

> brought to a halt by the sight at ground level of a great shapeless heap of low buildings topped by the outline [*silhouette*] of a factory chimney rising from its midst; here and there a lonely light flickered through a filthy window, five or six miserable lanterns were hung up outside on brackets whose blackened timber projected mysterious silhouettes [*profils*] like giant scaffolds, and, from the midst of this fantastic apparition, swimming in smoke and darkness, there rose a lone voice, the prolonged, loud wheezing of a steam engine exhaust valve, hidden somewhere out of sight.[13]

The day will dawn; the book begins; the reader, like Étienne Lantier, whose name will soon be given, will be told where this is and what chance there is of a job; and the novel will continue through this day and the next to unfold to the stranger and so to the reader the life of the mining district where he has arrived—that is, the conditions of daily existence for workers down the mines (they include some women) and also for the other women in the village, for the shopkeepers, and for the wealthy owners and managers and their families. Most of the details are based on Zola's preparatory reading and interviews; the novel provides, along the way, an education in all these many ways of living, across the social classes, that are associated with this one enclave of modern industrial life.

The novel will be driven by a strike that ends in defeat and a wretched return to work; it does not result in improved conditions or pay and there is no cross-class romance to offer a symbolic reconciliation of the kind that occurs, for instance, in Elizabeth Gaskell's *Mary Barton* (1848) or Charles Dickens's *Hard Times* (1854)—and also, but differently, in Zola's own novel *Au Bonheur des Dames*. At the end, Zola offers no simple way forward, and no immediate horizon of hope. In contrast, his last novel, *Travail* (*Work*) (1901), is open to criticism from the other direction. Like other much-read writings of the period, from Edward Bellamy's *Looking Backward* (1888) to William Morris's *News from Nowhere* (1892), *Travail* is unequivocally utopian in its vision of a coming society of industrial co-operation and contentment.

In the passage at the start of *Germinal*, we can see how Zola sets up an initial enigma—who is this man? Why is he walking and walking through the night?—with its partial elucidation proceeding alongside Étienne's own provisional view of the place he has now come to. From the stark contrast of the individual body against a vast unpeopled horizon, through the sparse information about who he is and his present situation of need, we reach the sightings of factory buildings and machines, half recognized and half perceived in the night-time unreality of the 'fantastic apparition'. The underworld of the mine itself will continue throughout the novel to be shrouded in this mythic quality at the same time as the reality of its passages and always ongoing work will be relentlessly described as well. Between night and day, on the edge of the mine and the edge of the novel, those 'profiles' and 'silhouettes' of what is half seen here capture not only the objective image of the way things do look at that time of the night but also a quality of the ominous and unspecifiable. Images—but real images—these outlines suspend the clarity of a full view.

Later in this novel, another *profil* will appear, along with a stark implied analogy. At the height of the strike a surging crowd, first women, then men, are moving across the field of view:

> Only their burning eyes and the dark holes of their gaping mouths could be seen as they sang the 'Marseillaise', and the verses tailed off into a vague bellowing, echoing to the beat of their clogs clattering over the hard ground. Over their heads, among the spikes of the iron bars that stabbed at the air, they passed an axe, keeping it upright; and this single axe, flaunted like the battle standard of the band, took on a the sharp profile of a guillotine blade against the light evening sky.[14]

Here the profile reveals not only the weapon itself but also its 'sharp' associations with the murderous aftermath of the French Revolution, almost a century before. So the profile's historical resonance, the clarity of its definition, intensifies the tension of the present moment. 'What dreadful faces!' says Mme Hennebeau, watching them as they pass. The wife of the manager of one of the mines, she has been taking a back route home from a day out with her daughters, one of whom, Cécile, had proposed that it would be fun to stop off for a glass of milk at a cottage. The word 'guillotine' now transforms them all into small-town modern versions of Marie Antoinette, playing dairymaids in their ladylike obliviousness to the plight of the workers who, in another echo of the Revolution, have been crying out their hunger—'Bread, bread, we want bread!'[15]

In the passage at the beginning of *Germinal*, the *profil* and *silhouette* are wholly visual, with the sight of them opening out metaphorically onto the ambiguities and uncertainties of the situation in this unknown place. Their many forms and shapes will be gradually developed in all their daily detail for both the reader and the primary character in a process of slow familiarization. In the description of the strikers wielding their axes, the profile operates through the placement of a straight historical connection, as much verbal as visual. That which is seen as a guillotine, nameable as such, points directly to the Revolution; it shapes the present image with that inescapable association.

## Experimenting with novels

A different kind of suggestive profile appears near the start of *Thérèse Raquin* (1867), like *Germinal* one of Zola's most famous novels. At first narrative sighting the heroine is presented as a nameless, unmoving figure confined to the space of a small shop in a lightless arcade. There is a comprehensive account of this *passage*—not one that you would go out of your way to look at, says the narrator, but rather a place that is used as a shortcut, with people in a hurry rushing through. This is followed by details of the shop—its deep windows and lingering stock of fabrics and bits and pieces of haberdashery, such as 'a heap of dull and faded

INTRODUCTIONS: CHARACTERS: PROFILES

objects which had doubtless lain dormant in the same place for the last five or six years'.[16] The description continues:

> Near noon in summer, when the sun's glaring rays burned down on the squares and streets outside, one could discern, behind the bonnets of the first window, the pale and serious profile of a young woman. This profile emerged vaguely from the shadows that held sway in the boutique. To the low forehead was attached a nose that was long, narrow, and slender; the lips were two thin marks of a pale pink, while the chin, short and nervous, was joined to the neck by a broad and supple line. You could not see the body, which was lost in the shadow; only the profile appeared, flatly white, punctured by a black eye open wide, and as if wiped out by a thick, sombre covering of hair. It was there, for hours on end, immobile and peaceful, between two bonnets on which the humid hangers had left rusty stripes.[17]

By keeping the profile—named three times—as its grammatical subject, masculine in French, the sentences build up an anti-naturalistic picture of a series of separate parts of the head and face. The rusty deposits on the bonnets have more signs of life than the young woman who sits there, motionless and yet 'peaceful'. It is a stunning introduction to the person who, it will soon be explained, despite having been a fairly wild girl, has passively gone along with her aunt's (and adoptive mother's) move from the countryside to this lifeless urban backwater. Thérèse marries the son of this Mme Raquin, her cousin—following, once again, the mother's plan.

The profile initially looks like an emblematic indication of Thérèse's two-dimensional existence as she endures the lifeless routine of a dead-end place where nothing happens (and little is sold). She is motionless, as if part of the dull display, a third

23

image between two hats for sale on either side of her; in the mode of a solid object she stays in one place 'for hours on end'.

Then some shocking vitality is injected into the unchanging profile, same place, same time, as it takes on a moving and uncanny life within the novel. The drama takes off with a passionate affair between Thérèse and her husband's best friend, a weekly visitor to the apartment where the other three live above the shop; this new pair then murder the husband, with Laurent, the lover, strangling him in a boat on a Sunday outing, then shoving him overboard to drown. The couple's crime is never so much as suspected. Instead, the old routine resumes after a while, with regular Thursday night guests, including Laurent. Ironically, the guilty couple get married at the innocent suggestion of the others. But they spend the rest of their days unable to rid themselves of remorse for the act they committed. Eventually they jointly commit suicide, haunted by the memory of what they have done. In retrospect, after the murder of Camille and the fraught restoration of seeming domestic order, that introductory profile—in the front of the novel, its shop-window starting pages—will come to have indicated something sinister.

When the novel was published in 1867 it was met with moral indignation and Zola responded with a self-justifying *Préface* for the second edition that soon followed (immoral as it might be, or precisely for that reason, the first printing had soon sold out). In this and in subsequent programmatic articles he used a proudly scientific vocabulary to claim that what he was doing in writing a novel was analogous to a medical experiment. Take individuals with specified properties, their 'temperament'; place them in a certain milieu, in given 'circumstances'; watch what happens, and write it up. The results, Zola suggested, might be informative;

he uses words like *étude* (study) and *enquête* (inquiry) to suggest an affinity with the newly developing methods of an accredited investigation or inquiry. If they were offensive to critics like those who objected to *Thérèse Raquin*, for instance, then that was beyond the responsibility of the researcher, who was simply reporting on what he observed. The author's experimental work was no different from that of a scientist in a laboratory; both aimed to add to the sum of practical, objective knowledge.

At one point in the *Préface* Zola used the stark analogy of the surgeon dissecting a body on the operating table: 'I simply carried out on two living bodies the analytic work that surgeons carry out on corpses.'[18] It is ostensibly meant as an indication of medical detachment and practical use, but it also has the effect of highlighting the sheer bodily explicitness of his novel. This comparison was amplified and repeated when Zola elaborated on his scientific rationale in a number of essays that were collected under the title *Le Roman expérimental* (*The Experimental Novel*) (1880).

The most obvious objection, logical if not scientific, to this clinical model of literary production is that whereas a fictional collection of characters is open to every kind of intervention—up to and including their creation in the first place and the conditions of the environment in which they are initially placed—that is not so in the real world to which the experimental findings are ultimately meant to extend. And in any case, authors can do whatever they want with a cast of invented characters—that is what it means to make up a story—whereas obviously there are no such powers in the world beyond the books. It is Zola—the narrator—who makes this happen, who pulls the strings that set the marionettes in motion; in the same way that, with all the powers of his authorial position, he is the one who initially set up the scene of the shop and the woman's profile as seen, every day. On occasion, Zola will acknowledge this difference himself by stressing the active and essential element of authorial creativity within this framework. The novelist has to 'see, understand, invent', and it is some specific observation of theirs that will 'spark the idea of the experiment to set up or the novel to write'.[19]

Yet if the theory of novel-writing as a scientific experiment was clearly tendentious, it got people arguing (it still does). And so it helped to sell the books. That success, and the surrounding controversy, are relevant to the whole history of the reception of Zola as an author who was well aware that negative criticism could be turned to one's advantage. His first job was in the publicity department of Hachette, at the time an enterprising new Paris publishing house—and still a name today as a major international consortium. From the beginning, then, he knew the vital importance of marketing. And he also knew how it was done; he was attuned to the new techniques of promotion, *la publicité*, that not many had yet grasped in theory, let alone in practice. It is not by accident or mere talent that his first fictional publications—*Thérèse Raquin* (1867), *Madeleine Férat* (1868), and before them *La Confession de Claude* (1865), and the stories collected as the *Contes à Ninon* (1864)—sold well and were widely noticed and reviewed. Their author knew how to make that happen.

In light of what is now the conventional separation of the sciences and the arts, the choice of the experimental model seems not only wrong, demonstrably, but also quite strange. Why would you want to liken a writer's work to what a scientist does in a laboratory or what a surgeon does in the operating theatre? There is surely not much in common between the individual invention on one side and the methodical diagnosis and medical procedure on the other.

But for Zola, there is. The convergence or at least comparability of science and modern art was exactly what he wished to suggest and to bring about in his own practice as a writer. He did really see himself as engaging in research; in the preparation for writing each of the novels in the Rougon-Macquart cycle, that was precisely what he did, with the field trips to locations and other preparatory work. In this sense there was method, a recognizable and frequently repeated procedure that was directly derived from the collection and recording of data in the real world.[20]

In another way too Zola's theory of novel-writing as a scientific experiment is just like a widely deployed twentieth-century practice with regard to the modelling of human responses in specified settings. In the postwar decades, long before AI became the talking point of the mid-2020s, computers were already set to enable the realistic simulation of consumer behaviour and thereby to enable the planning of marketing strategies in accordance with likely responses. Just like Zola's model of the elements or characters that will react against one another in a given medium or milieu, so here the results are dependent on the variables and instructions that are initially inputted into the system. It seems reasonable for a marketing expert to hypothesize about typical behaviours in using a language of technical objectivity; in that context, the scientific frame is exactly what is sought and expected. In a comparable way, Zola was deploying what he took to be a form of objective credibility for his own constructions of likely social types.

And advertisers, just like novelists, are prone to the invention of would-be realistic character types that, given the distance of half a century and more, may appear anachronistic or eccentric in the light of a now later version of likeliness. Take this double invention, for instance, in an essay about likely tyre purchases from a 1960s American collection on *Modern Marketing Strategy*: 'the probability of buying new tires after six months is one thing for the salesman who drives his car five days a week, but something quite different for the little old lady who drives her car only to church on Sunday'.[21] Plausible or not, selective types have their own effects in setting the terms for the perception of a given social milieu and its characters, in its own time and afterwards. If Zola wanted novels to be scientific, then this is where science becomes novelistic.

## Sex in the shadows

Zola's very first novel, *La Confession de Claude* (*Claude's Confession*) (1865), is charged with a concentration of emotion that is unlike anything to be found in his subsequent writing. Yet it also involves scientific elements in the form of a brutally forensic self-analysis on the part of the first-person narrator. Claude is consumed with possessive jealousy with regard to his mistress, Laurence. As he waits for her in their lodgings, he cannot restrain himself from imagining that she stopped off on her way out to visit her former lover, Jacques; and when she does come back he cannot help pouring out his impassioned obsessions, along with bucketloads of their history, all the way on to his fears for the future:

> I came up to Laurence, I took her in my arms, speaking softly, in her ear, my voice caressing and apologetic. I don't know what I

said to her. My heart was full, I emptied it. My speech was a long prayer, ardent and humble, gentle and violent, full of pride and humility. I handed over the whole me, in the past, in the present, in the future; I produced the history of my heart, I delved down into the lowest parts of my being so as not to hide anything. I needed to be forgiven, I also needed to forgive. I accused Laurence, I asked her for loyalty and frankness, I told her how much she had made me cry.[22]

And so on, and on. What sets this apart (just about) from the emotional extravagance it recounts is the narrator's separation as he describes the psychological mechanism in which he is caught—and which implicates, all the time, the other person who is its relentless object. Divided into irreconcilable polarities of guilt and innocence, gentleness and violence, Claude pushes each side alternately onto the other person, whose non-responsiveness only draws attention to himself as the source of it all. Possessiveness is experienced in the form of its reversal, as if it is him who is taken over. There is some comedy too in the appallingly simple emotional economy: 'my heart was full, I emptied it'. The speaker is watching his own absurd performance at the same time as he is completely caught up: as if looking on but unable to stop it all pouring out.

When Laurence falls asleep, her passivity first becomes that of a dead body, inert and impassive and all the more insecure as Claude physically grasps her:

> And here I was clasping to my breast just a corpse, just something unknown that was foreign to me and whose meaning I could not penetrate. Oh! brothers, you have no idea of this suffering, these spurts of love that knock against an inanimate body, this cold resistance of flesh you would like to melt into, this silence in

response to so many tears, this deliberate death that could love, that one is beseeching with all one's power, and that doesn't love.[23]

The narrative compulsion—the stories that must be told, and the forgiveness that must be sought or offered—then moves into regions of more violent fantasy. Laurence's heartbeat is heard as the sound of a machine that is functioning well, 'the movement of an unconscious clock',[24] a functional attribution that can transform it into an object for dissection:

> I would have liked to take the machine apart, to go and look at it so as to study its smallest pieces; in my madness I was seriously thinking of opening up this breast, of taking this heart and seeing why it was beating so gently and deeply.[25]

He imagines Laurence's heart telling him that she is about to leave him, going back to her life on the streets. There she 'would die one night, on the pavement, drunk and drained' and be taken to the amphitheatre for dissection.[26] The scene of medical investigation becomes a graphic extension of the narrator's obsessional fantasies of crime and reparation as the brutal moral examination of a forced confessional is transposed, *in extremis*, into a postmortem.

*La Confession de Claude* dramatizes the tortured and torturing self-division of a young man whose story, in one straightforward sense, is within the conventions of the nineteenth-century novel of apprenticeship, the *Bildungsroman*. He has arrived in Paris from the provinces—from Provence in the south—and his 'confession' is framed as letters to the college friends he has left behind—those 'brothers'. Zola's own situation, during part of the time when he was writing the book, was not unlike this. Born in 1840, he had

## INTRODUCTIONS: CHARACTERS: PROFILES

grown up initially in Aix-en-Provence and had moved—with his mother—to Paris at the age of seventeen (his father had died when he was seven). He maintained a correspondence with two close friends from school, one of whom was none other than the painter Paul Cézanne. In this connection, the profiles and silhouettes to be found in the early writing can be seen as indicative of a visual aesthetic that would be a constant of Zola's work, from the painterly detail of many of the novels' descriptive passages to the regular writing of art criticism. One of the Rougon-Macquart novels, *L'Œuvre* (*The Masterpiece*) (1886), is about an artist.

But the blurred vision of *La Confession de Claude*, part of the anxious indeterminacy that pervades that novel, has little resemblance to the confident gradations of Zola's later character-drawing. During the night of his lurid imaginings Claude is leaning out of the window, looking across into the lodgings of his friend Jacques, who may or may not be with Laurence. Eventually, some clarity emerges:

> two profiles, enormous and energetic, appeared in outline, detaching themselves with clarity and vigour. You might have thought that the shadows were tired of tormenting me and had wanted finally to reveal themselves; there they were, black, powerful, with a superb truth and insolence. I recognized Laurence and Jacques, outsized and disdainful. The two profiles approached one another slowly, and they united in a kiss.[27]

With that insistent image of the operating table, Claude then likens himself to a patient enduring the final 'sensation of agony' at the hands of the surgeon: 'I suffered so as to suffer no more.'[28] The horrible confirmation with the merging of the profiles has given the spectator (within the story) the satisfaction of a proper dramatic climax: 'That was the only reality, the dénouement at once demanded and feared.'[29]

From another point of view, this spectacle of the familiar couple's dreaded embrace has some features of the fantasy that Freud would elaborate as belonging to a universal childhood experience. In the 'primal scene' the child—who wants his mother to himself and for whom the father is a usurper—is witness to what it does not understand as the sexual union of the parental couple, with the father violently possessing the mother. With Claude, as with other situations of these early novels, another man has a prior claim to the woman he loves, who is his own first and exclusive love.[30] In the novel, the melodramatic excesses of the entire situation continue to proliferate as Laurence's sick friend Marie, also present in the room with Claude, is called on to corroborate his interpretation of the shadowy evidence before promptly dying (yes, dying!) in his arms. Through it all drives the demand for 'truth' and 'reality', at least as Claude sees and seeks them: the demand for the closure which, even as it represents the actualization of his worst fears, can be named as such, in the abstract, as a dénouement.

## Social problems

The excesses of this first fictional protagonist are interesting precisely because they are so far out of line with the styles of Zola's later novels. Apart from the self-absorption, unmatched by anything else he would ever publish, *La Confession de Claude* is unusual in Zola's œuvre in that it was written off and on, across a number of years (he began it in 1861). For the rest of his life Zola's practice, unfailingly, was regular and systematic. His novels were planned out in detail before being written. There was method and habit in the making up of the notes and outlines from which the text would be produced, just as there was in the period of writing itself. This steady working method was also a conscious philosophy of how to live. The Latin tag *nulla dies sine linea*—'No day without a line'—was framed above the fireplace where he sat and wrote in his study at home.[31] And this was exactly how Zola lived, with a steady output of several pages every morning. Thanks to the plans, he always knew where he was going. Writing was an occupation, a job of work. He almost never flagged; on the contrary, he thrived on the work and was lost without it. One lucky chance, as we shall see, of many months living by himself in England in the late 1890s was that it coincided with a moment when he had a novel all ready to be written. That gave him something to do—and something to keep him sane.

The early Paris years were a training for this working practice as well. From the job with Hachette Zola moved into mainstream journalism, writing weekly columns and reviews on politics as well as on art and books and plays.[32] He was able to experiment with different strains of writing, including some brilliant satirical pieces, and he was also establishing himself as the controversial critic who would later become the leading figure in a radical new literary movement called naturalism (for which that *Préface* to the second edition of *Thérèse Raquin* was a kind of manifesto). It is worth stressing too that for Zola, the marketization of literary work was not a development to be deplored, nor was such work to be set apart as belonging to its own world of art for art's sake, *l'art pour l'art*. In a powerful trio of articles called 'Money in Literature' ('L'Argent dans la littérature'), which were published in 1880, he would sketch out a history of that relationship, from the age of patronage to the present.[33] For Zola, modern arrangements of work and payment represent a liberation from feudal forms of dependence.

The articles Zola wrote during these first working years are remarkable for the variety of their styles and topics, and also for the consistent power of the writing itself. Not only does he produce a daily quota of lines, but the lines are always worth reading. Take, for instance, a pair of polemical reviews written the same year that *La Confession de Claude* was completed. It is the early autumn of 1865 and Zola is intervening in an ongoing controversy, prompted by recent productions, about what counts as valuable in a new drama. Not yet himself an established novelist (or for that matter a dramatist, as he would soon begin to be, with a stage adaptation of *Thérèse Raquin*), he begins to formulate the principles that will be repeated again and again in defence of his own works and those of like-minded colleagues. He explains how the unpopularity of Émile de Girardin's play *Les Deux Sœurs* was attributed to audiences thinking its plot was too much like a tabloid story, a *fait divers*, just transposed into dialogue. 'Nothing wrong with that' is effectively Zola's retort. Such real-life stories, 'human reality', contain everything needed for a theatrical treatment; the problem is that they get distorted into blandness when converted to fit the prevailing theatrical conventions.[34] A dramatist like Girardin is doing something different, Zola says; he is 'tired of the smooth skills of the day, tired of the banalities, and he wants to attempt the study of the big social problems on stage'.[35] In other words, what Girardin has produced, unlike what is expected, is both true to life and useful in the real world. These *faits divers* are inherently dramatic material in any case: 'there is a fertile source of emotions and action in the study of social problems arranged as a drama'. And Zola adds a vital amplification to this: that these issues are 'studied in the life of each day, in the relationships people have with each other'.[36]

The review is already close to the programmatic statements that would soon be formulated as Zola's working assumptions as a writer of fiction. Human 'reality' is the appropriate subject matter for novels, not some stylized literary or theatrical version of it. Within that large domain, the specific focus is on what he calls 'the big social problems', a markedly modern and practical specification of that reality. 'Social problems' implies not a static picture, but a process. There is the technical expertise of a 'study', a 'diagnosis', and, implicitly, a horizon of remedy, enabled by the justice of the exposition and the fact that it is shown at all. It is notable too that this large perspective can be seen and tackled through concentration on the small elements of 'the life of each day'. This is not a matter of abstraction but about showing the details of a social problem on the ground—in a real-life exemplification. Worth noting as well is that the stress on the social does not preclude or exclude the assumption that 'emotions', along with action, are also required as an element of the drama. So the short passage encompasses the full range of focus between, on the one hand, the broad picture of society as a whole—a problem must be identified and tackled as a general issue—and on the other the miniature, ethnographic description of the details of everyday life in a given time and place. All of Zola is already there.

ÉMILE ZOLA

## Sexual observations

'Human reality' seen in the form of 'social problems': this is will be future for Zola's writing career. During this first period Zola also wrote in defence of *Germinie Lacerteux* (1865), a controversial novel by the brothers Edmond and Jules Goncourt which featured a decent servant girl secretly leading another life. In the daytime she faithfully looks after her invalid employer; at night she slips out to engage in a wild and unhappy life of sexual excess. This wayward behaviour is given a biographical explanation, as being the result of abuse; that is, it is not presented as an inherent character fault or a sin, but is rather associated with an event in the woman's life over which she had no control. That event, in turn, is identified with the sort of experience likely to happen to an ignorant girl who has recently arrived in Paris. In all these respects, then, *Germinie Lacerteux* is a case study, bringing out the social—and socially sexual—sources of one person's wretchedly unhappy way of keeping going. It is in these terms, including the reader's own perspective, that Zola presents it in his review:

> We are present at the agonizing sight of a loss of human nature; we have before our eyes a certain temperament, rich in vices and in virtues, and we study what phenomenon is going to occur in the subject coming into contact with certain facts and certain beings. ... I feel the unique curiosity of the observer.[37]

Later will come the explicit elaboration of the experimental analogy, making a naturalist work like the staging of a medical trial: you set up the characters and the situation, and watch what happens. That scenario is present already in this early piece of journalism, but seen from the point of view of the reader or the critic, not the creator. The stress on the curiosity that goes with being in that position—as, elsewhere, on the curiosity of the writer—is vital too. Just as the situations for representation are typically charged with strong emotions in their responses, so their observers, before and after, are not supposed or intended to be indifferent.

In *La Confession de Claude*, the work of the would-be young writer in his lodgings is interrupted by the arrival of the destitute Laurence, who (through no fault or action of her own) takes over his every waking thought, as well as his space. When she eventually departs (and the dying Marie is usefully dead as well) Claude is able to announce that 'I was free.' Apart from the need to deal with the body of the good woman, still in the room—'I had forgotten Marie whose peaceful head was resting against my chest'—he can concentrate now on converting his experience into a tale of warning for future young men not to ruin their youth with the wrong sort of sexual initiation.[38] He abandons Paris and packs himself off back to Provence and the fraternal companions who have been the nominal addressees of what is formally a one-sided epistolary novel.

Zola did have a brief period of living as a penniless writer, but there was no return home from the poverty and corruption of the capital to the childhood familiarity of Aix. Instead, his writing would move away from the concentration on a single masculine consciousness; that self-absorbed persona would turn out to have been a singular exception in the enormous fictional output that followed. Claude leaves Paris behind, never to return; Zola stays put but abandons the solipsistic self-analysis. All his life, Zola would continue to work—to write—at home, just as his Claude had tried to do. But the choice of the people he looked at and wrote about would no longer be confined to those he might hope to make out in the shadowy, merging profiles on the other side of the courtyard. They would be just about everybody.[39]

In *La Confession de Claude*, the narrator is haunted by the thought of Laurence's previous attachment to his friend Jacques—haunted by images that can waver between hallucination and actuality, since Jacques lives in the very same building (so that Laurence really can just pop in there on her way out). In all Zola's early fictions there is a preoccupation with the significance of the first sexual partner; the first love is the vital love, and it colours all subsequent relationships. This applies to men as well as to women; it is not a version of the usual Victorian double standard, which sets a value on the virginity of unmarried girls (and condemns them for the loss of it), but is tolerant of the variable sexual behaviour of men. Hence Claude's protestations at the end of his lament: he feels he has ruined himself and he wants his experience to serve as a warning to his 'brothers' not to fall into the same trap. It is not only that Laurence herself first belonged to Jacques; it is that he, Claude, will always, throughout his life to come, have been Laurence's lover before he was anyone else's.

In those first three novels, in other respects very different, the virtual presence of a woman's former lover is an insistent theme. If he can't be observed from the window, moving about in shadowy possibility (as in *La Confession de Claude*), then he will be dead but enshrined in a portrait distractingly hung in the bedroom (*Madeleine Férat* and *Thérèse Raquin*). In all three of them, moreover, the two men concerned have grown up together, so that their own connection is close in a way that is independent of their relationship to the woman they have in common. To that extent the link is on the verge of being incestuous, and that is reinforced by the closeness of the domestic setting: Claude and Jacques as residents of the same building, Thérèse's two husbands first alternately then successively occupying the same bed with her (and thus with each other) in the apartment above the shop.[40] In *Thérèse Raquin*, the (second) couple are overseen in the bedroom by a portrait of Camille, the first husband, which was painted by none other than Laurent, the second husband. In *Madeleine Férat*, Guillaume has a photograph of his old friend Jacques in an album. After he reads of the shipwreck that has apparently led to Jacques's death—and before he knows that Madeleine, who now lives with, him, was previously with Jacques—Guillaume has this picture framed and hung up on their bedroom wall. In this novel Jacques does return, not dead after all—and Madeleine, now married to Guillaume, feels compelled, and against her own desire, to sleep with him once again. In the same way Claude's suspicions of Laurence turn out to be justified: she really is with Jacques again. The case of *Thérèse Raquin* is the most extreme, since Laurent has actually murdered Camille to get him out of the way; yet from that time on, the new couple's passion is at an end. Their crime is never exposed, but (until they decide, in desperation, to kill themselves) they are doomed to go back to Thérèse's original life of domestic confinement and unfulfilment, from which the passion of their affair had once been her release. The bedroom portrait, and the guilt, are always there.

*La Confession de Claude* is concentrated on the one narrative of its self-obsessed central character, who stays where he is in the room from which he obsessively watches to see what might be going on in another part of the building. There is no space here for other possibilities, aside from the dream of return to the open air of the Provençal countryside and the easy intimacies of boyhood companionships. But in *Madeleine Férat* and *Thérèse Raquin* the tragic or melodramatic tones are tempered by the comedy of other perspectives. In these novels, Zola is trying out his narrative repertoire, and plays with the possibilities of presenting characters who either fail to pick up on what is going on right in front of them or else allow others to think them oblivious when in fact they can see it all.

So in *Thérèse Raquin*, some time after the terrible death of Camille, Mme Raquin's beloved son, the household returns to its weekly evenings of card games with a few old friends who, in flat-character sitcom style, can be relied on to repeat the same kinds of laboured comment every week. Laurent, will be of the party as before, and from these occasions comes the suggestion that it would be only natural for him, as an old friend of the family, to marry the young widowed Thérèse. Then, in the gradual decline of the period subsequent to their wedding, it is made clear that Mme Raquin herself, now in need of constant assistance and assumed to be mentally incapable (she can no longer speak), has eventually understood, from unguarded remarks of Thérèse and Laurent, what really happened. She tries and tries, when the guests are there, to communicate her realization via the basic writing through which she makes known her everyday needs—and over and over again, the message fails: too long, too complex. She can only look on as eventually the guilty pair make up their minds to take their own lives—and hers.

Mme Raquin is desperate for an incriminating truth to be revealed to the world and duly punished. In *Madeleine Férat*, with another frail old person, M. de Rieu, we have something like the full comedy counterpart of this situation. Unlike Mme Raquin, this witness has no wish to impart what he sees—or any wish for it to be understood that he notices what he sees at all. Something between a voyeur and a detective, he takes his pleasure from the secrecy of observations that are themselves undetected and unsuspected because of the pose of doddering incapacity that he maintains. M. de Rieu's entertainment comes from watching his wife, Hélène, who is younger than he is but much older than the very young man, Tiburce, with whom she is having an affair. This attachment is described with clinical specificity as 'the mad passion of a woman who has reached the change of life and who, at this critical moment, rediscovers the excitations of puberty'.[41] An extreme and early example of Zola's classificatory leanings, this withering menopausal diagnosis is remarkable—in the late 1860s—for its open and semi-technical reference not only to women's sexual desires also but to life-stage variations in their intensity. At another point he describes the manner of Madeleine's sex education at school, how 'In the corners, behind the leaves of some hedge, she came upon groups talking about men; she joined in these conversations, with the ardent curiosity of the woman awakening in the child, and this was how she received her precocious life-education.'[42]

Mme de Rieu's affair with Tiburce has been going on for years; before that there was always a troop of local boys hanging around the house, with her husband well aware of their presence and purpose:

> On occasion... M. de Rieu would penetrate into Hélène's room in the morning and keep her panting there for an hour as he chatted away about the fine weather and the rain, while some innocent boy would be suffocating under the covers that had been hastily pulled up on the husband's unexpected entrance.[43]

By operating what amounts to a kind of suspension of belief, as if none of this had anything to do with him personally, M. de Rieu is able to both attend and extend the bedroom farces being performed in his very own home. Ostensibly in the position of the idiot cuckold, in reality he is able to control the action himself, both creating and enjoying his own domestic drama.

Tiburce had initially arrived as a lodger when still at school, and now hangs on in the house with the hope of getting a job in Paris, where Mme de Rieu has contacts in the right quarters. What he does not know is that her husband keeps blocking her efforts when they are on the point of success; and this, with its regular sequel of Tiburce's violent rages, becomes a continuing source of entertainment for M. de Rieu. A scene towards the end of the novel displays the dynamics of this comically complex *ménage à trois* by having both the wife and the lover simultaneously pour out their complaints to a seemingly sympathetic interlocutor of the same sex. The three of them are spending the evening at the unhappy home of Madeleine and Guillaume in Paris. As is the custom, the men have moved into another room after dinner, but M. de Rieu, as an invalid, stays behind with his wife and Madeleine. He is taken for deaf as well as stupid so that his presence is no impediment to his wife making use of the opportunity to confide her woes to another woman; 'she took the deepest pleasure in her sufferings'.[44] Meanwhile, in the adjoining room, Madeleine's husband is on the receiving end of an equivalent monologue from Tiburce:

> He began to smoke furiously; then, after a short silence, he let himself go with the rage that was smouldering in him. He made his confession to Guillaume just as his mistress was making hers

to Madeleine, but with a crudeness of expression that had a different kind of energy.[45]

Zola is always attentive to gendered differences of behaviour, so clearly demarcated here by the ritual separation of the sexes for their own conversations after dinner. The topic is the same, but the style and the words to say it are not. Zola does not quote either of the two narrators directly, so that the episode is not just a comedy but also a commentary on the divisions that are being played out here.

The strange knowing figures of M. de Rieu and Mme Raquin in these two novels can also be seen as surrogates for the all-knowing narrators of these and other fictional stories. Instead of being non-existent or purely a writing convention, these are solidly present individuals, within the story, who witness the confessions of other characters, if not the events themselves—to their own amusement (M. de Rieu) or distress (Mme Raquin). The position of such characters then suggests further questions that draw in, at either end, both author and readers (like us). The author seems to delegate and thereby to draw attention to aspects of his own control or knowledge, while readers are disconcertingly or else amusingly presented with characters who, like them, are observing the action without being thought to be capable of intervening in it. We are shown not just a story but the circumstances of its setting up and its telling. The handling of a story by its producers and consumers—who gets it to happen, and who can react to it—becomes a live issue within the novel itself; it is not simply given, at a safe narrative distance.

In his critical writings, from the beginning, Zola clearly asserts the value of innovation: a real artist should always be trying to do something different, to push at the boundaries of the expected and the conventional. His own later way of working, with the careful preparation and the daily output, can make it appear as if he himself was anything but such an artist. But it may be that that perception comes from what is itself a received idea about the difference between creative and conventional writing. Zola's genius—it seems to me—was that he combined that consistency of production—his sentences never stumble—with a real commitment to finding new fields for the novel. The project of the Rougon-Macquart cycle, first sketched out in 1868, the year *Madeleine Férat* was published, was an experiment on a grand scale. But in the novels that precede it, Zola is trying out different modes of fictional narration and subject—alongside the apprenticeship and accomplishments of the prolific journalistic and critical writings that he was producing throughout this time.

## Roles

Lastly, let us look at a later example of Zola's experimentation with character types. *Une page d'amour* (*A Love Story*) (1878), the eighth Rougon-Macquart novel, is set in Paris and like *Madeleine Férat* combines comedy with a focus on the psychology of falling in love and also, in this case, the social and literary conventions that surround it. In the earlier novel there was a distinction between, on the one hand, the mockably silly minor characters—the household of the de Rieus—and on the other the suffering, struggling couple of Guillaume and Madeleine who are the primary focus. But here the comedy, in some ways even more farcical, develops a different kind of edge when it takes in the central characters too.

The heroine of *Une page d'amour*, another Hélène, is a young widow in Paris with a frail little daughter, whose life is saved one night by the ministrations of a neighbouring doctor, Henri. Hélène becomes friendly with Henri's wife, Juliette; and in the customary contrast of character types, Juliette is set up as the distracted, flirtatious counterpart to the thoughtful, devoted Hélène; as one of her ongoing diversions, Juliette is hosting a production of Alfred de Musset's light play about adultery, *Le Caprice*. So far, so novelistically conventional. The theme of the play being put on by the characters is suggestive of what might or must not go on in the unfolding story; but Henri and Hélène, though falling in love, are persons of principle, unlike Henri's wife—and so they may not succumb. When the morally upright Hélène learns of an assignation between Juliette and another man in some sleazy rented rooms that she knows about, she feels torn as to what she should do. In the end, she leaves Henri an anonymous note with the time and the place—but then, regretting that doubtful move, she goes to the place herself at the appointed time, where the transgressive couple, uncomfortable with each other and not quite yet *in flagrante*, are grateful for the warning and hasten to leave by the back stairs. Cue the arrival of Henri who, finding Juliette in the place and at the time specified by the unsigned note, of course assumes that this is her way of offering herself to him at last.

The whole comic sequence is played out with superb narrative timing, further enhanced by the seedy setting. Zola relishes the precise description of interiors—especially when, as here, they have been deliberately constructed within the story: as an overdone stage set for a seduction. First Juliette, and then—in the next scene, after she has left—her husband, reflect on the tacky décor. It is Juliette's thoughts, spoken out loud to her would-be lover, which stall the seduction, while Henri will wonder how Hélène has come by such an unlikely place. What is shown, then, is not only the predicted results of the brilliantly orchestrated confusion—what *Zola* sets up—but also the way that the characters themselves react to the likely scenarios suggested to them: how they interpret the rented rooms as a low-budget stage set meant for the enactment of a specific series of events. They know just where they are, in terms of an expected story—and that awareness, involving resistance and mild disgust, is part of their experience.[46]

It is not often that Zola will grant his characters a happy ending, even in the short term. In this instance, Hélène, who began by seeking to stop a wife from committing adultery, now goes with the flow of the scene she finds herself in with the husband of that same woman. By acting with moral initiative, she is granted her own resisted adulterous consummation instead. But then the aftermath of this comically choreographed outcome is movingly unexpected. Zola does not go into the details of the lovemaking, but 'When Hélène came back in her bare feet to fetch her shoes in front of the dying embers, it occurred to her that never had they loved one another less than they had that day.'[47] And there the chapter ends.

# 2

# MILIEUX IN THE MIDDLE SHOPS

## Shopping milieux

All the novels of Zola's middle writing period, in the twenty-strong Rougon-Macquart series, are grounded in specific social and historical settings, and their people and stories follow from those. The *milieu*—literally, the middle—is fundamental to Zola's sense of what shapes characters' ways and what prompts or enables particular kinds of action or plot development. Brian Nicholas put this eloquently: 'Zola is not concerned with excusing the individual or examining the question of freedom, only with dramatizing and making irrefutable a relationship—the interdependence of the individual with the forces which play on him in a particular situation.'[1] With a changed milieu, the story and the people would be something else.

Out of all the many milieux that Zola covers, this chapter concentrates on one that is itself, by definition, in the middle. In a shop both customers and commodities are in transit, passing through. They arrive, then they leave; the point of purchase is en route between the place of production and the place of consumption. Zola was intensely conscious of the significance of shops, both in everyday life and sometimes as hubs of creative innovation. The prime location for looking at Zola's shops is naturally the novel of 1883 that is named after one, *Au Bonheur des Dames* (*The Ladies' Paradise*). There he dramatized and drew out in the greatest detail the mechanism (his word) of a new kind of large-scale city commercial enterprise, the department store.

But shops are also casual meeting places where people drop in all the time to pick up their daily supplies and exchange a few words. And while *Au Bonheur* has rightly received a great deal of attention for its display of the inner workings and imaginings of the new large-scale commerce of the late nineteenth century, there is more to shop history, and more to Zola's own representation of shops, than just the big stores and the one shopping novel. Apart from the main store, there are numerous small shops to be found, here and there, including within the pages of *Au Bonheur* itself—shops that vary in their capacity for keeping up their existence in the face of the challenger big store, as well as according to what kind of goods they sell. Often, and not only in the stand-out *Au Bonheur*, Zola's ordinary shops are much more than a subordinate part of the setting; they play an integral part in the story, significant in the lives of their customers or their personnel, and sometimes also, as with *Au Bonheur*, in relation to a larger and longer history of retailing practices.

It was the shops that started off my Zola-reading life in the 1980s, drawing me into a PhD about nineteenth-century consumer culture and its literature. *Au Bonheur* was the centrepiece of that dissertation, and of the book it became, *Just Looking*. In this chapter I will be talking about others of Zola's many shops as well. But *Au Bonheur* remains the focal point for what I find most appealing and distinctive about Zola's way of writing. For me it is the primary exhibit in Zola's œuvre. As students change, and as shopping itself continues to evolve in the wider culture, it yields something new with each reading and each teaching. Surprising new angles are always appearing, and unexpected items are found stashed away on forgotten pages.

At the same time, department stores look different now that they are themselves a dying form of commerce rather than the harbingers of a new commercial modernity of fashion for all (as they were in Zola's time), or the representatives of leisurely, ladylike shopping that they still were forty years ago. As recently as the 1990s there were constant trips to the Knightsbridge Harvey Nichols department store in the cult BBC sitcom *Ab Fab—Absolutely Fabulous*—and that real-life store was opening a superb new branch in Leeds (in 1996).[2] But that moment now, in the 2020s, looks like a glamorous last attempt to bring new life to a mode of buying and selling that was on the verge of losing its appeal. For the internet was coming, and the department stores had pretty much had their day.

The narrative of *Au Bonheur* is all about the dramatic new force of the department store and its social meanings. By the time you have read it, you know all about the workings of what at the time was a just invented marketing idea: sell every category of goods in one single vast store, on several floors, and sell with low profit margins in order to maximize sales and turnover. So thorough and accurate is Zola's exposition of the operations and inventions of this new mode of commerce that the novel is an established reference for retail history in its various disciplinary dimensions—architectural history, labour history, feminist history, and business history, for instance. That is to say, this work of fiction is regularly treated as a historical resource. Yet it is only in recent decades that the study of consumer culture, including the history of shops, has become a significant and now quite extensive academic field, one that is cross-disciplinary by nature—taking in not only history of every kind but also psychology and geography and sociology, to name a few more. In the beginnings of that development, an important book was Michael Miller's 1981 study of the founding period of the Bon Marché department store—the store where Zola had done most of his own research, a century before, for the writing of *Au Bonheur*.[3] It is as if all shopping research paths, all the retailing roadmaps and once futuristic shopping superhighways, were bound to lead back to Zola and Zola's totemic department store.

Historically, the department store stands out as the great innovation, the shop on an industrial scale, after which all other shop types, henceforth defined as both small and specialized, acquired a different kind of identity, if they survived at all. In that sense, the department store comes from and contributes to a historical moment that is comparable to our own, with online shopping now apparently in the process of installing a new retail paradigm, in relation to which every pre-existing kind of shop then has to adjust or refit itself. The same quasi-Darwinian language of a struggle for survival is active, just as it was in the late nineteenth century with the arrival of department stores (and the then recent arrival of that Darwinian language, too); and again in the middle of the twentieth century when supermarkets and self-service became the default mode of food retail.

If shopping is changing in our own time now, then so is the way that we understand previous shopping worlds as well, including that of the department store. For with many of them having now closed down, it may not be long before even those great big shops will be needing a footnote to say what they were: how everyone used to visit them once in a while; how they had their origins in the late nineteenth century, particularly in Paris, and that this is beautifully documented and dramatized in a novel of 1883 by Émile Zola. As for the other shops, not just the department store, perhaps in the not so much further future it will be necessary to explain to prospective readers that there was a time—a long time—when people bought almost everything that they did buy from stores located in actual buildings, which they had to visit in person in order to make the purchase. That footnote might go on to say that in France the ultra-local routine of daily food shopping survived for longer than it did in most other Western countries, and did so even in the biggest cities, and even in the face of that country having invented the seemingly so un-French phenomenon of the *hypermarché*, bigger than the biggest of supermarkets anywhere in the world. Even so, though no longer the only or even the primary source of food purchases, the local neighbourhood or *quartier* maintained a role, with the *boulangerie*, for instance, holding its ground as the source for daily bread. In France, by the time online shopping arrived, there were also still many regular open-air food markets in towns and cities of every size.

*Au Bonheur* stands out not only because it gives such a full picture of a department store but also because, for the first time—in fiction or any other prose writing—it is itself a presentation of retail history. By showing and analysing the change in modern commerce—he calls it a revolution, no less—Zola helped to create the sense of that history: that this was the appropriate language for what had been happening, that a change in the shops should be represented as a significant part of modern history. That itself, in retrospect, was a kind of a small revolution, and one that brought women's history, in all its dimensions, to the fore.

From the outset, then, Zola's novel about a department store has been treated as a regular source for the history of shops and shopping, nothing to do with literature. But there is also the question of the place of this shop-novel within *literary* history, and in relation to Zola's work as a whole. Where does the prime shopping novel sit within the ranks of all Zola's other novels—on their own, or else in their various connections to one literary debate or another? How does it relate to the fluctuating fortunes of these novels as texts prescribed, or not prescribed, on course syllabuses in schools or colleges—and bought, or borrowed, or read, in that other dimension that we call 'for pleasure'? In those connections, much more nebulous in reality than the metrics that are meant to apply to some of them, I would hazard a guess that there has been—to put it summarily—a slow-burning shift in the past few decades from *Germinal* to *Au Bonheur* as the best-known, or at least the just-about-heard-of, novel by Émile Zola. He wrote about shopping, didn't he? Instead of: There's a novel about a miners' strike, isn't there?

Or to put this differently: whereas previously the mention of Zola might have brought up a thought about the full-on realism of the late nineteenth-century novel, with this genre being associated with the hard facts of heavy industry, and sweat, and poverty, in the last few decades there has been a gradual movement across to the lighter, service side: to shops and leisure. Labour history has declined, along with the industries themselves (in Europe at least) that it studied; the so-called—stupidly called—'gritty' realism of the nineteenth century is out of academic fashion today. But feminist history has taken over where the heavier forms of now male-seeming labour history left off. Zola's picture of the department store is not only about the invention of a leisure industry; it also goes into the micro-politics of a mixed workforce and a struggle against harsh conditions of employment. Added to this, a novel about the invention of a shopping destination, with all its attendant dramas on both sides of the counter, can seem as contemporary as any twenty-first-century online start-up. To put it more bluntly, when the mines shut down, the vintage department store opened its doors, welcoming in a whole new Zola readership. Also, a small-screen audience: in the twenty-first century the novel has inspired two long-running TV serials, *The Paradise* and *Il paradiso delle signore*—one based in England and one in Italy.[4]

These adaptations also prompt a pre-emptive warning about how *not* to read *Au Bonheur*—or how to get over what's bad about it. I need to do this in part because the recent versions have given the impression that the novel is primarily a sweet Cinderella story in a sumptuous upmarket setting, complete with ugly sisters in the form of bitchy superiors and rivals who are all satisfyingly tamed or ousted by the end. In this soap-ready story, the lowly and somewhat saintly Denise Baudu arrives in Paris with nothing and then, without even trying to, wins the heart of her otherwise somewhat ruthless employer, Octave Mouret, the princely philanderer who marries her at the end. In the manner of every virtuous or feisty heroine, from Samuel Richardson's Pamela to Jane Austen's Elizabeth Bennet, Denise refuses to consent to the kind of agreeable affair that is Octave's expectation; nor does she think she even likes the man much. He is an imaginative entrepreneur but a heartless boss. But by the time he does finally offer marriage, her good feminine influence has brought about most of the needed welfare reforms in the store; it is she who reigns, as the novel repeats many times in its classically epithalamic finale.

But it's not that bad; it is even possible that the fairy-tale veneer is in part a device that enables a more radical and more modern feminine identity to slip in unobserved. For despite the novel's ending, Denise Baudu is no mythical heroine; she has qualities that look forward to twentieth-century feminist revisions of that role more than back to her more passive precursors, and in many ways she is an unlikely object of princely desire, one that does not fit the mythical paradigm. She arrives in Paris with two younger brothers; thus she has dependent children but is not their mother, which in conventional terms reinforces her virtuous qualities rather than making her into a sexually fallen woman. Instead she is a self-reliant, and gains Mouret's admiration by her articulate talk about the new commerce and what is required to improve its working practices. Virtuous as she (really) is, she talks back and talks with intelligence (she is *au courant* with the latest theories of retail marketing). She has none of the alluring sexuality of the heroine of *Nana* (1880), Zola's novel from three years before about a working-class Paris girl who becomes a celebrity actress and high-end prostitute, reducing her wealthy lovers to (graphically described) states of abject erotic enslavement.[5] She is also promoted within the store to running a department of her own; and she is not the only woman to hold such a position there.

## Within the arcade

But before any thought of radical social or personal change, there are the shops that are bound up with continuity, with the slower time of everyday life. These small-scale shops of *le petit commerce* are the stores that are just there, as if timeless, providing a steady livelihood, and with the likelihood of passing the business on within the family: in Zola's time that was most often from father to son, or else to son-in-law, the long-term apprentice who will have married the long-suffering daughter. Such a shop caters to the predictable needs or small luxuries of equally modest lives; its regulars enter and purchase and leave, perhaps with a few moments' chat as well.

*Thérèse Raquin* is a perverse illustration of the shop as this kind of non-event. In it, a shop's premises are the main scene of action, and there is an extreme example of the intra-familial business marriage since Thérèse, the shop-owner's adopted niece, has married her cousin, the shop-owner's son. But in this novel almost no attention is given to the shop as such. For this very reason, it is a kind of counter-example of a shop-novel hardly about shops at all; at the opposite extreme from the show of *Au Bonheur*, the store and the novel, in which shops and their history and futures make up the whole world.

Published in 1867, *Thérèse Raquin* comes before the twenty Rougon-Macquart novels, and unlike them it is not located at a specific historical moment. Instead, from the opening page, a narrator speaking as though with an intimate conversational voice, here and now, sets a scene of vagueness and abandonment. We are shown a dingy Paris *passage* which is only used as a shortcut and where, 'A few years ago', at certain times of the day, that profile of a young woman was visible through the grimy windows of a fabric shop patronized only by occasional customers who went there out of habit.[6] The static setting suggests a timeless and lifeless long existence for both the shop and the arcade, with its collection of lustreless businesses. Apart from this *mercerie*, the only one singled out consists of a large cupboard or *armoire* on the other side of the passage from the shops, out of which an old woman sells trashy jewellery. Other shops have cast out old things onto the flimsy shelves of other *armoires*: 'nameless objects, goods forgotten since they were put there twenty years ago'.[7]

This introductory section gives a fairly detailed description of the stagnant retailing environment behind which almost all the events of the novel take place, from the feeble gas lighting in the evenings to the exact layout of the shop interior, as if giving instructions for a stage set. But everything of moment occurs upstairs, in the living quarters; even the entrances and exits of the clandestine lover on his afternoon visits to Thérèse take place via an external staircase, also meticulously noted in the opening chapter. The shop itself, in this novel, is more like a front for the main action, the drama of adultery and then murder and the long aftermath of that. Through it all, and beyond, the shop persists, as a place and a business. It retains the visible aspect of torpid tranquillity, upstairs from which a sequence of shocking events takes place—which, at the time of the narrating, have happened but are now covered over, once again, by the arcade's familiar semblance of stagnation.

This faded thoroughfare has none of the sense of dialectical temporality that Walter Benjamin would see in that suggestive cross between street and interior, outside and inside, as it appeared to him in the middle decades of the twentieth century. In their first period, several decades before Zola's novel, the city arcades had been a new architectural invention, a covered walkway with shops on either side and living accommodations above them, enticing the unhurried city stroller to stop and look and perhaps to shop; at that time they had been at the forefront of new developments and new ways of conceiving the uses and pleasures of urban space.[8] But in *Thérèse Raquin* the *passage* is just what the word might imply, no more and no less: a crossing as just a way through. The narrator goes out of his way, as it were, to make this clear, declaring authoritatively that 'The Passage du Pont-Neuf is not a place where people go for a stroll. It is a short cut, a way of saving a few minutes. Those who pass through it are busy people whose sole concern is to get where they are going as quickly as possible.'[9] In other words, not a *flâneur* to be found. The slower, more leisurely approach is indicated, repeatedly, but by negation. Instead the rationale given is one of functionality, of people in transit, dashing through, for whom time and space are resources to be saved and estimated: the shorter the better, whether in distance or minutes.

The rapid movement of these passing persons is unconnected with such shops as are there; Zola stresses their mental detachment from their momentary surroundings:

> All day long there can be heard the same irritatingly irregular patter of footsteps hurrying along the passage; nobody ever stops to talk; everyone goes quickly about his or her business, head down, at a brisk pace, without so much as a glance at the shops. The shopkeepers look anxiously at any passer-by who, by some miracle, happens to stop in front of their window [*étalage*].[10]

Wonders will never cease—a customer! That 'irritatingly irregular' clacking of steps transfers the perspective to that of the shopkeepers, looking (and hearing) from within the shops. In the context of such lethargy the real miracle may be that they bother with anything that can be called a display—an *étalage*—at all. Strange shops!—and it *is* the shops, collectively, that are invoked, not just the one that will turn out to be the truly weird site of the narrative that follows. The reaction reinforces not just the passivity but also the perversity of these people. As shopkeepers, they might be assumed to welcome and foster the transformation of a passer-by, a *passant*, into a customer; that is what an enterprising shop with an attractive frontage is supposed to be for. But here, the first stage of that alteration provokes not hope but anxiety.

The dark dissuasion of the displays in the *passage* is brought out by an unlikely but directly contrasting scene further into the novel, where a wholly non-commercial place does just what those shop displays don't. At this later point Laurent, Thérèse's lover, is going to the morgue every day to look out for the recently drowned corpse of her husband Camille. In the morgue there is always a mixed crowd, all sorts, such as young working women 'who went from one end to the other of the glass screen, slowly, eyes wide open attentively, as if they were in front of a fashion store's display'.[11]

The shop in this simile is a *magasin de nouveautés*, a new type of establishment and a precursor of the department store. Literally 'novelty shops', selling new or fashionable things, these places were notable for their vast plate-glass windows. The glass of the morgue has the attracting effect that the arcade's small shop windows do not; more generally, the analogy implies that an absorbed looking into shop window displays is a typical phenomenon that can serve as a template for a different situation. For the visitors, this is explicitly a *spectacle*, a show that is free of charge and open to all, with every social class represented among the gazers. Yet unlike a shop window or a play, its producers have no control over the content. Some days it is plentiful, 'a fine display of human flesh', but on others there may be nothing at all, and then 'people go away disappointed, feeling they have been swindled, and muttering between their teeth'.[12] But they come, all the same, to see what's on offer: this morning's mourning. Gruesome or gorgeous, the demand is there for something exposed or exhibited through glass.

The simile of the fashion shop or *magasin de nouveautés* stands out not only in relation to its pointed contrast with the real business of the morgue but also because of this novel's indifference, for the most part, to varieties of shop or shopping experiences, despite the primary setting in an arcade and the primary involvement of the main characters in a family-run boutique. This apparent absence of interest is all the more noticeable in the light of *Au Bonheur des Dames*, published sixteen years later, an entire novel not just about a shop but about nothing else. In the later novel little boutiques of comparable stagnation to the ones in *Thérèse Raquin* are located not so much in a timeless back *passage* as out there on the novel's front line as time-limited: marked or fated for imminent demolition, to make way for the encroaching *grand magasin* of modernity.

ÉMILE ZOLA

# In the big store

In Zola's time department stores were a new kind of interior public space, in which women could spend time engaged in a new kind of open-ended activity, which was shopping. Everyone, anyone, could come in and look around these grand new stores, enjoying the displays and the opulent ambience, without being expected to have any definite object of purchase in mind—as was the case with the traditional, smaller shop, dedicated to just one type of goods. Marketing strategies are directed at the constant creation of new desires in the women who pass through its doors—or who simply stand and stare at the wonderful window displays outside, which draw them as if inevitably into the orbit of the store. *Au Bonheur* begins with precisely that scene, as the novel's main character, Denise, just arrived in Paris, is instantly, magnetically drawn to the extraordinary *vitrines* of the big new store—as though that new kind of marvel were the first of all sights to be seen in the modern city.

Alongside its transformation of shopping, and shoppers, the department store is shown in Zola's novel as a new kind of workplace, with women as well as men behind the counters. They are attracted by the beautiful environment but also suffer from precarious conditions of employment, such as annual lay-offs in the low season. By covering a period of several years in the course of the novel, Zola is able to show positive progress towards more enlightened working conditions, in line with reforms that were beginning across Europe in other large enterprises at the time. This is as much a novel about labour history and shopworkers as it is about the development of a significant new cultural form designed to appeal to women with time, if not necessarily much money, to spare. The store, in both cases, will draw them in—to work in it and to want what it offers, the merchandise and the place.

*Au Bonheur* is the Bildungsroman of the store that its title names; the human characters, the workers, the owner, and the customers of every class and type, are all subordinate in comparison, placed in relation to this great overarching phenomenon. And insofar as the novel is one example of Zola's distinctive documentary style, with each in the Rougon-Macquart series presenting a portrait of some distinct micro-milieu of the Second Empire, it is surely the most detailed and comprehensive of them all. A reader of *Au Bonheur* receives a complete education in the organizational workings of a big store like this in the late nineteenth century, getting to know it from the shopfloor up and the dormitories down, as well as via the staff and customers on either side of the counter. There is discussion of the labour issues involved for a numerous and diverse workforce with strong seasonal variations of turnover—and the introduction, over the time of the novel, of various reforms, from pensions to pay levels to job security. There is a sense of the significance of the department store for its clientele, in making a place where women can come to spend free time in the city, with shopping now a new kind of leisure activity. Equally, there is the creative passion involved in the production of this new kind of environment, both at the day-to-day level, to make it an always surprising place where women will want to come, and in relation to the planning of special events, so that there is always something else to see—in promotional terms, something not to be missed.

There are also precise elaborations of specific new selling strategies, both aesthetic and practical, most of which have been standard in most retail environments since, so that what is striking now is to encounter them in their first appearance as unfamiliar practices. These range from fixed prices, with labels clearly displayed (there is no need to ask, but also haggling is not allowed); to the right to return unwanted goods, thus removing a reason for hesitation before a purchase; to the commission system as an incentive bonus for persuasive assistants; to in-store customer facilities, from restrooms to cafés to reading rooms and art displays.

Over and above all these separate elements is Zola's repeated inculcation of the basic business model, in keeping with the scale of the building itself and the multiplication of departments and types of merchandise. Stated simply, the operational principle of the store's success is low profit margins offset by fast turnover. It is the same principle that animated all the mass merchandising of the subsequent decades and centuries—including the twentieth century's practical sequel to the glamorous, leisurely department store: the supermarket.[13]

The department store's *vitrines* are the visible—and transparent—indicators of what is new and different about this kind of retailing space. In the opening scene of *this* novel, the shop windows are shown to be irresistibly attractive, this time in the marvelling eyes of a provincial but fairly retail-savvy young woman (she previously worked in a dress shop). This is Denise, at the point when she has just stepped down from the train, with her brothers in tow. From the visual magnificence of the grand design, down to the minute appeals of a quality bargain, amazing spectacle, and amazing deals, everything about this store is extraordinary to Denise, and placed at the front of the novel to provide a first-time customer's reaction to the building that is to be its focus. Seeing the own-brand 'Paris Bonheur' silk displayed outside, with its rock-bottom price clearly marked, she exclaims, like the speech bubble of a cartoon advertisement, 'Oh! That black silk fabric at five francs sixty!'—with the narrator adding, as though in a quiet footnote for equally inexperienced readers, that 'exceptional articles' of this type are going to 'revolutionize the business of fashion'.[14] What they are is what twentieth-century marketing jargon would name *loss leaders*: in order to draw the customer in to buy other products as well, the store sells a given item at a price below what was paid for it.

That fashion market, *le commerce des nouveautés*, is literally 'the novelties trade', novelties being a catch-all term for new stuff being sold; it is the micro level of specific commodities that corresponds to the macro level of the department store or *grand magasin*—'big store', literally—that sells everything and anything. In this new shopping world, saleability takes precedence over any other feature; specific uses and needs give way to whatever will count as *the latest thing*: as fashion, as new. That 'the fashion market' is even a thing, let alone a thing that has a history, and a revolutionary history at that, is implicit in the narrator's comment, at least as important as the many facts and facets of the new kind of store that are being introduced for the first time in the novel. It is the very newness, in the nineteenth century, of the emphasis on newness itself which both enables and promotes the development of that special new category of retail specialization which is *nouveautés*—novelties.

In its larger picture, this revolutionizing of the selling of fashionable goods is a shake-up of retail itself. From now on, although they may continue to trade, perhaps just as they did before, the shops of the old and established type will be differently situated because the broader context has changed. And that is the drama that is directly played out in *Au Bonheur* through the conflict between the aggressively expanding department store and the consequently struggling little shops of its neighbourhood. The windows of Denise's uncle's shop are not just dull or dirty, like the ones along the arcade in *Thérèse Raquin*; more than that, they can only be seen and described in their negative contrast to the sparkling vitality of those of the Bonheur. Again and again, like a hopeless Homeric epithet, the *vitrines mortes* or 'dead windows' of Baudu's shop are called by that dooming name, shown up as the outward sign of the shop's now inevitable failure in the face of the competition across the way. 'Just in front of her, the Vieil Elbeuf, with its rusty façade and its dead windows, seemed to her so ugly, so wretched, looking at it from her vantage point of luxury and life';[15] this comes at the point when Denise is applying to work in the rival store across the street. Or on a later occasion, right after Denise has been sacked from the Bonheur, 'the Vieil Elbeuf seemed dead behind its dark windows'.[16]

## Sexual pressures

*Au Bonheur* presents its retailing development—or revolution—from all points of view. The drive and inexorability of the new commerce are matched with equal vigour and passion by the counter-movements for labour rights and the efforts of local shopkeepers to fight back; the deliberate and cynical manipulation of women's desires and behaviours is collectively and individually matched by the palpable enjoyment of new pleasures and satisfactions and opportunities for women as both shoppers and employees. Over the course of the novel there are numerous small stories and sketches involving particular customers and shopworkers, highlighting the kinds of connection that are fostered by this distinctive store environment: between colleagues, or between assistants and customers. On show at these moments is Zola's great gift for pinpointing the complexities of a social situation by means of a tiny, telling scene.

In one exchange, for example, he brilliantly dissects expectations on both sides of the counter from the points of view of a wealthy customer, Mme Desforges, and the male assistant, Mignot, who is helping her try on pairs of gloves:

> Half lying on the counter, he was holding her hand, taking her fingers one by one, slipping the glove on with a long caress, repeated and firm; and he was looking at her, as if he had been waiting for her face to show the signs of a voluptuous swoon.

The assistant is disappointed in the lady's lack of reaction to an experience that is a turn-on for him, in part because of the powerful odour of the material which, so the narrator says, she too, when at home, finds arousing. 'But in front of this ordinary counter she did not feel the gloves, they did not produce any sensual heat between her and this random sales clerk doing his job.'[17] Between them are not just the formal, categorical differences of class and sex but also their incommensurable experiences of these. For the sales clerk, what he is dealing with is a woman—or is to be reduced to that. On the woman's side, and this is made explicit, it is quite otherwise:

But she, her elbow on the edge of the velvet, her wrist raised, lent him her fingers with the tranquil air with which she was used to presenting her foot to her housemaid, for her to button her boots. He was not a man; she was using him for intimate purposes with her familiar disdain for the people who worked for her, without even looking at him.[18]

For her, 'He was not a man' because he is a servant; and for him, she is not superior because she is female. It is a scene of transient anonymous intimacy that can go unremarked in the shop environment that creates and enables it, just as each of the parties to it is oblivious to the other's understanding of it (their indifference, in one case). After Mme Desforges has moved away from the counter, Mignot reprises the incident as if it had happened according to his fantasy, with a wink and a 'crudely' explicit one-liner to a colleague.[19]

Zola narrates another charged incident involving inequality of power between a man and woman, this time between two employees and with far more than a momentary fondle at stake. It is a case of full-blown sexual harassment, almost a century before that form of workplace exploitation would be given a name, with the potential for calling it out officially. Denise finds herself left behind in the staff cafeteria, on her own with the ex-army official whose job it is to police the behaviour of both workers and customers. She knows he may well report her and get her sacked on the pretext of having seen her in a part of the store where she shouldn't have been, and she has also learned, as part of the female culture of the place, that he is liable to try to trade sexual favours in exchange for his non-reporting of workplace misdemeanours. Here is the ensuing brief scene, told from Denise's perspective of mounting fear. He blocks her exit from the room:

> And he came closer. Now she was completely scared. Pauline's words came back to her; she remembered the stories that were going round, of salesgirls terrorized by old Jouve and having to buy his goodwill. In the shop he was content with little familiarities, such as gently patting the cheeks of obliging girls with his big fat fingers, taking their hands in his and keeping hold of them as if he had forgotten they were there. It stayed fatherly, and he only let loose the rampant bull elsewhere, if you accepted the kind invitation to buttered *tartines* at his home, on the rue des Moineaux.[20]

Coming back to her at this moment of heightened fear, the man's relatively innocuous harassment takes on the menace of the full assault. Then, as predicted and feared, he does indeed press Denise to come over for *tartines*; she refuses, and manages to fight her way out, only after shoving him back off balance. Shortly afterwards, when he has duly reported her, she loses her job.

The subtlety of Zola's narrative skill here works partly through the identification he creates between the reader and Denise. But he also conjures up a whole workplace culture in which women tell each other about specific men and in which a level of ostensibly harmless interference is at once registered (by the women) and allowed to pass (because it can appear accidental or insignificant). All the shared knowledge that has been imparted to her by her colleagues comes flooding back to Denise at this moment of terror when she is entirely on her own with the predatory man. It is an extraordinarily complex representation of the mechanism of sexual harassment.

## Local ambitions

*Thérèse Raquin* and *Au Bonheur* represent the two extremes of Zola's depictions of shops, chronologically and in other ways. In one, the shop is barely there, an emblem of small stagnation; in the other it is a symbol of a vibrant new leisure culture in the later part of the modern century. But between the two, in size and significance and in Zola's own writing, there are many more types of shop.

These local or otherwise small-scale shops are part of everyone's lives, and Zola shows that too. There are shops to be found in just about every novel. Even, say, in the largely shopless environment of *La Joie de vivre* (*The Bright Side of Life*) (1884), where their presence is nonetheless a part of regular routines. The butcher and the baker visit to press for overdue payments. Pauline goes every three months to Caen, the nearest big town, to go through a list of errands and purchases that she has been compiling methodically during the intervening period. The flat statement of this, unbrightened by examples, seems only to add to the novel's atmosphere of unvaried confinement. We stay with the preparatory admin rather than enjoying a change of scene. This may be a day spent away from home, but it is not a source of diversion for Pauline.[21] The shops and markets are a hinterland here; they do not figure in any strong way but are noted, all the same, as essential elements in the rhythms of daily and quarterly life. Zola is that rare writer for whom this part of ordinary reality does get transferred into his representations of that life.

Elsewhere, on the other side of the counter, he attends to shop-making ambitions, and in the rest of this chapter we will look at two middle-sized establishments, both of them local but also changing. One is from *L'Assommoir* (*The Assommoir*) (1877), where the heroine, Gervaise, opens what is initially her own laundry business, and the other is from *Le Ventre de Paris* (*The Belly of Paris*) (1873), is a delicatessen in the area around Les Halles, the great Paris food market. These modest developments are as modern and imaginative in design as the innovations shown in *Au Bonheur*, but they have suffered from the neglect of the middle—squeezed out of the sphere of critics' attention to make way for the more spectacular manifestations of the department store, above all, or else at the other extreme for the dull destitution of failing or faded shops—in *Thérèse Raquin* or in *Au Bonheur* itself, where the big store is taking away their trade.

Local shops, like large ones, can be deliberately set up as attractive spaces, with the goods they offer being not only regular purchases but also meant for special occasions, or wished for and saved for as marks of a certain level of security and status. For *L'Assommoir*'s Gervaise, a desire for social advancement takes the form of the wish to have a business of her own, together with longings for special items to furnish a home. She dreams of having a laundry business, and dreams of possessing a mantel clock; she gets both, and later loses both, in the novel's symmetrical matching of entrepreneurial and acquisitional aspirations.[22] In *L'Assommoir* there is nothing like the department store's unbounded feminine desire and the deliberate generation of that by marketing design. Wants and longings have distinct objects—like the clock or the shop. They may be associated with a modicum of material improvement, even luxury, but they are reasonable, and within reach.

In *L'Assommoir* Zola gives us a picture of the understated but ubiquitous place of shops, in a local urban world that abounds in retail and service and manufacturing outlets of numerous kinds. Consider, first of all, the moment when Gervaise gets her own premises and sets up a laundry. The business flourishes, and so does she. In this passage we see her in her local element, her happy milieu, at this point in her life when everything is going along beautifully, and she can be oblivious to ongoing family tiffs:

> In the middle of all this backbiting Gervaise, tranquil, smiling, at the entrance to her shop, would be greeting friends with a friendly nod. She liked to put down her iron for a minute or two, to smile on the street, with a shopkeeper's surge of vanity, when a bit of the pavement is hers. The rue de la Goutte d'Or belonged to her, and the nearby streets, and the whole neighbourhood.[23]

In the middle of everything, family quarrels, the work going on inside the laundry, Gervaise as the manager can take her 'minute'—her me-time—to enjoy this sense of proud possession. All mine, the street and, by implication, the shop itself, with the threshold a joining rather than a boundary, and the physical surge or *gonflement* all part of the symbolic expansion that it implies. If the emotion is typical, not personal, that is no diminution or deflation; it is the confirmation of having arrived. She is where and who she wants to be, and that achieved place is identifiable as that of a woman running her own business. But she is also one of the workers; the roles and the spaces all overlap, without conflict.

The passage continues with Gervaise appreciatively surveying the larger picture of a street that is a whole world: 'a look to the left, a look to the right, at both ends, to take in the passers-by and the houses, the pavement and the sky';[24] she appraises in detail the separate shops and workshops that can be seen from her door, differentiated by what they sell and by how much they show of that or themselves or their cats. There is 'a huge grocer's' with a display of dried fruits; there is a fruiterer's and a tripe shop; she exchanges a friendly nod with the coal merchant (a woman); there is an umbrella shop whose windows are dark, its door closed, and its mother and daughter shopkeepers never seen; opposite are a blacksmith's, an ironmonger (female again), and a fast food outlet, a woman selling fried potatoes.[25] The long appraisal is comforting and comfortable.

Beginning with the phrase 'The neighbourhood thought Gervaise was really nice', the next paragraph complements her own view, describing the local admiration that is now by consensus granted to this woman and her good hard work as a member of her own team. A little later, the same theme is taken up in relation to Gervaise as a customer, another aspect of her integration within the community: 'In the neighbourhood she had ended up being regarded with a lot of respect because, really, there weren't a whole lot of customers that were as good as she was, paying straight down, not nit-picking, not moaners.'[26] A list of all her preferred shops follows, with names and addresses. 'She got her bread at Mme Coudeloup's, rue des Poissonniers', and so on, including the butcher, the grocer, the wine merchant, and the coke merchant (in twenty-first-century style, she has negotiated a special tariff with her fuel provider):

> And it was certainly the case that the shops she patronized served her in good faith, knowing there was everything to be gained

with her by showing themselves friendly. So when she was out in the neighbourhood, in slippers and with her hair loose, people said hello to her on all sides; she was still at home, the nearby streets were like the natural dependencies of her lodging, which opened straight onto the pavement. Now she would sometimes let an errand take longer, happy as she was to be outside, with the people she knew all around her.[27]

And on the days when she doesn't have time to cook, she picks up a takeaway from the *traiteur* with the dirty windows across the internal courtyard of her building.

In light of the miserable later phases of Gervaise's life—her roofer husband Coupeau will become a drinker after his accident, and later so will she—these are poignant passages. Against expectation, Gervaise has achieved ambitions that were always directly articulated as such—the noun *ambition* and the verb *ambitionner* are frequently used. She has worked hard, she has planned and calculated, and she has done it. And now the leisurely tour of the shops she patronizes is like a minor triumph, a progress among the subordinate *dépendances* of the nearby streets. At the same time it is utterly casual, no need to dress up. It is a friendly exchange among equals, the sign of belonging. And again, as when she stands in the doorway, there is no hard border between Gervaise's actual boutique and its natural extensions outwards to the other shops and streets.

This permeability of boundaries—between shop and street, and also between the roles of manager, worker, and customer—can be seen as well in the blending of interior space between the business and the living quarters, and this is where we come towards the more comic aspect of the set-up. The laundry is at the front, the living area behind it. But a back room gets used as storage space, and there is always an easy to and fro as household members move about from one part of the premises to another. There is nothing odd about that; this kind of combination is the standard arrangement for shops, going back to the customary absence of separation between home and workplace before large-scale factories and office buildings established that division as the norm. In addition to the shops, *L'Assommoir* also has instances of outsourced homeworking, in particular Coupeau's censorious sister and brother-in-law, the Lorilleux, who work together all day long in their lodgings, performing some obscure process with valuable metals.

All these various spatial and practical blurrings appear as such only in light of accustomed divisions from later periods, themselves now once again diminishing with the advent of what has come to be called (in English shorthand) WFH: working from home. But the shop on the rue de la Goutte d'Or has one further feature which points in a striking way towards key future features of some small-scale retail while linking this, brilliantly and comically, to a parallel development in the case of one of the characters. What I have in mind is the transformation of this particular shop unit each time it changes hands—it has no fewer than four different incarnations over the course of the novel—and the corresponding evolution of Auguste Lantier, Gervaise's former partner, who returns to the area and moves in there during her own occupation of it. (This Lantier is the father of some of Gervaise's children, including the Étienne Lantier who is making his way towards the mining village at the start of *Germinal*.)

When first encountered, before it belongs to Gervaise, the shop had been a *mercerie*, selling fabrics. With Gervaise and her husband Coupeau, it is a laundry. Then when Virginie Poisson and *her* husband move in, it changes again, now to a fancy grocer's, even though Virginie is herself by training a laundress like Gervaise. At the end, with the prospect of yet one more handover, to another couple, the place is set to be converted into a *triperie*. It is as if it could be anything; there is no sense of an established speciality, whether for the shopkeeper or for the space. And each time it changes hands and changes use, the place gets a makeover, most dramatically in its post-laundry identity:

> After some hesitations, Virginie had decided on a small fancy grocer's, with sweets, chocolate, coffee, tea. Lantier had argued strongly in favour of this kind of business, on the grounds that there were enormous sums of money to be earned in gourmet delicacies. The shop was painted black, with touches of yellow, two distinguished colours. Three carpenters worked for a week setting up the drawers, the windows, a counter with shelves for the jars, as in luxury confectioners.[28]

With characteristic attention to detail, Zola gives the specs for every aspect of the job—for the merchandise, the labour (or part of it), and the decorating. There is a chosen colour scheme, with a suggestion of special thought on the subject. And there are fixtures and fittings installed with a team of skilled workmen. The attentively planned design of the shop space is to complement the type of goods to be sold there, little luxuries.

In human terms, there is also the comedy of Lantier, the man, being played out here, alongside the small tragedy of Gervaise's humiliation, as the displaced tenant. Lantier's commercial advice to Virginie is the comfortable consultancy of a man who is never moved to do any physical or other kind of work in the course of the novel and yet who remains or becomes an ever more solid fixture in the shop, as if part of the furniture—in this case, the only furniture that stays where it is. He is initially installed in one of the back rooms as a lodger added to the Coupeaus' household. He pays no rent and also becomes Gervaise's lover (or original husband restored); she visits him in his box room while Coupeau sleeps. But when the Coupeaus move out, Lantier stays, keeping his room and quickly establishing the same sexual arrangement with Virginie, whose husband works nights. As lodger plus lover he comes with the territory, as if part of his own business plan. He is even a fixture within the selling space of the shop:

> For a year he had been living on nothing but sweets. He opened the little drawers, never mind the losses, when Virginie asked him to mind the shop. Often, in the middle of a conversation with five or six people there, he would take the lid off a jar on the counter, stick his hand in, and munch on something; the jar would stay open and was emptied. No one took any notice of that any more, a mania, so he said. Then he had thought of a constant cold, a throat irritation, which he talked about soothing. He still did no work.[29]

Lantier takes what he wants and does what he likes; he neither pays nor works. He gorges himself as a sort of on-site consumer-shopkeeper, as if unconditionally entitled on both sides of the counter at once. And he kings it with his new non-wife, even persuading her to hire Gervaise back as a cleaner of her own former premises. For Gervaise, in true tragic style, 'It was a last levelling, the end of her pride.'[30] Lantier, meanwhile, 'huge and fat, sweating the sugar he nourished himself with', continues to feed off the place, which duly starts to give off 'an odour of ruin. Yes, he had only a few wafers left to nibble, a few bits of barley sugar to suck on, to clean out the Poissons' shop'.[31]

After the Virginie interlude, when Lantier has managed to eat her out of house and home, the show is all set to go on. The Poissons are being evicted, and he has been 'hanging around the daughter of next door's restaurant, a magnificent woman, who was talking about setting up as a tripe seller. Get that! People thought it was funny, they were already picturing a tripe business installed in the shop; after the delicacies, the solid stuff'.[32] From clear-out to start-up, or sweets to solids, it is the oscillation of a precariously balanced diet (and of signature heavy-handed Zolian symbolism). It will 'keep' Lantier exactly where he wants to be.

The revealing perversity of Lantier's position is not only that he sticks it out and sucks it up all along, whatever the individual qualities of any given shop or woman. It is also that what he gets out of the ongoing arrangement, unspoken but as if serially renewed, has nothing to do with monetary gain—he puts his hand in the jar but not in the till—even though its effects on the others concerned, in the losses sustained by Virginie's shop, are the same as if he had actually stolen the stuff. Single-handed, as it were, he causes the failure of the shop, but he is the only element of its environment that outlives its transient set-up as an *épicerie*. Like the bricks and mortar, Lantier stays put and putty, eternally malleable to the retail model of the moment. Other than that, he has no fixed identity; or rather, his identity consists in its continuing flexibility in relation to the variable particulars of his place of entitlement, as contentedly consuming non-paying lodger with benefits.

## Modern retail style

Finally, here is one more shop, from one more novel, this one bringing a settled prosperity for that type of consciously modern local business started by Virginie in *L'Assommoir*. It is a spic-and-span new *charcuterie*, situated next to Les Halles in *Le Ventre de Paris* (1873), as set up by the lovely Lisa Quenu, 'la belle Lisa', and made possible by legacies that she and her husband have separately received. Zola describes this place with a connoisseur's precision, writing it up in a way that amplifies the attention devoted to the shop's design:

> Lisa spent hours with the workmen, giving her opinion on the minutest details. When she was finally able to install herself behind her counter, people came in droves to buy from them, just to see the shop. The walls were completely covered in white marble facing; on the ceiling was an immense square mirror framed in a broad gilded cornice, richly ornamented, from which, in the middle, hung a four-branch chandelier; and behind the counter, along the entire wall, on the left, and at the back, more mirrors, caught between the marble panels, created pools of brightness, gateways that appeared to open out onto other chambers, *ad infinitum*, all of them full of meats laid out on display. On the right, the counter, very large, was singled out as a beautiful piece of work; lozenge-shaped pieces of pink marble made a design of symmetrical medallions. On the ground the flooring was tiles of alternating white and pink, with a dark geometric border.[33]

Until the mention of the meat display, the *viandes étalées*, it would be hard to guess that these immaculate surfaces and multiplying mirrors were the setting for a food store, let alone one for which blood-oozing black pudding is the weekly special, lovingly prepared on the premises by the store's extended family all together, including employees, pets, and children.

As with the successive refurbishments in *L'Assommoir*, what we see here is the start of the trend that produces shops themselves as smart generic spaces, distinguished by their aesthetic modernity as much as by the category of merchandise they sell. The fully developed department store, in which every type of commodity is sold in the same impressively beautiful building, is just around the historical corner. Meanwhile, this new shop is a source of pride for its local neighbourhood as well as its owners—and that, in a neatly circular economy, is itself a draw: people keep on coming to buy there, just to have a look. The place has its own pull; or put another way, the point of sale is itself a selling point, with that appearance of tautology reflecting the magnification effects of the many mirrors. Again in anticipation of those that will be on view in the much larger real space of Au Bonheur des Dames (the store), and in the pages of *Au Bonheur des Dames* (the novel), these mirrors, placed at all angles, display of display, are a repeated feature, carried over between the two shops and the two novels.

Here again, Zola goes over the premises with an attention to detail like that of the shop's new owner. But Lisa's vision is also expansive: 'the young woman dreamt of having one of those light modern boutiques, sumptuous like a drawing room, with their mirrors reflecting the brightness out onto the pavement of a broad street'.[34] *One of those* indicates that this kind of shop can already be pointed out as a modern type, giving Lisa the template for her dream, which is imagined in such minute detail that (like Virginie with her new sweet shop in *L'Assommoir*) she is able to supervise the workmen while it is being actualized as a light promotional space. For it all comes true. And the shop prospers, except for the temporary upset caused by its association with her brother-in-law Florent, who returns from wrongful exile, and is ultimately deported a second time for alleged anti-government conspiracy.

At the end of the novel, with Florent now out of the picture once more, his position as semi-outsider is taken over by Claude Lantier (not to be confused with his father, Auguste; this is a brother of Étienne), who will in due course get his own novel as the artist protagonist of *L'Œuvre* (*The Masterpiece*) (1886).[35] Lantier, who so far in *Le Ventre de Paris* has been seen occasionally as a supplier of unsolicited aesthetic tweaks to shopkeepers' displays, is brought forward at the end to pronounce a damning repudiation of domestic-commercial contentment—*le bonheur*—as enjoyed by the likes of *la belle Lisa*. Zola gives Lantier's verbatim snarl at decent folk, *les honnêtes gens*, as the novel's own last words. But before that, as witnessed by the disgusted artist, we are shown the recovered peacefulness of Lisa's morning routine—even including, these days, an exchange of greetings with her erstwhile rival Louise, *la belle Normande*, who is now installed in her own ultra-modern establishment, a classy tobacconist's and wine shop.

That calm and settled contentment of standing in front of a shop of her own is what Gervaise found, for a moment; it is what Lisa too wants, and wanted. It is the *bonheur*—the 'paradise' and the happiness—of having got as far as the place you had knowingly longed to reach, a zone of both comfort and joy, radiating its local connections. Au Bonheur des Dames, 'the ladies' paradise', is the name Zola chooses for Octave Mouret's store, where feminine satisfactions of every kind are to be created and marketed to the customers who visit it. In *L'Assommoir* and *Le Ventre de Paris* women's shop-happiness is equally at issue, but here the emphasis is on the pleasure for women who are running the businesses themselves rather than for those who are coming to them as customers. They are the ones who have made it.

Lisa Quenu has known her own moderately ambitious mind from the start. Her super-rich speculator cousin Saccard, the protagonist of Zola's preceding novel, *La Curée* (*The Kill*) (1872), serves her as an image of what not to be or want to be when she sees him driving around in his fancy carriage, looking unhealthy and unhappy: 'as for making money just for the sake of it, and giving yourself far more bother making it than you get pleasure out of it afterwards, well, I'd rather just sit back'.[36] For all the proverbial dressing of this declaration—money for money's sake? What's the point?—it is striking that it is stated in the form of a cost–benefit calculation, weighing up the relative quantities of the trouble endured as opposed to the pleasure enjoyed as a pay-off. The more modest philosophy of a small and stable satisfaction, and self-satisfaction, is also a trader's best estimate.

*L'Assommoir* and *Le Ventre de Paris* both showcase experiments in shop-making identified by their initiators as *modern* and as a means to their personal fulfilment, an outlet for small-scale but precise commercial ambitions. It is vital, too, that so many of the principal shopkeepers in these local establishments are women. Given the dominance, in all senses, of the male owner Octave Mouret in discussions of the department store and the exploitation, or enablement, of its overwhelmingly female clientele, it is easy to miss this feature of the smaller concerns. Even Mouret's predecessor, the first wife from whom he inherited the smaller

Au Bonheur des Dames before building it up, was a woman. The talented and articulate Denise is promoted to running her own department over the period covered in *Au Bonheur*; other departments, beginning with the one in which she first works, are already headed by high-powered, confident women. In the big establishments also, then, there are opportunities for a bright young woman. A smaller shop, for those with the skills and the means, was a way of working for yourself, often from home, and of acquiring a local status. It could also be creative.

Zola saw this. He saw too the way that a shop engenders specific roles for all parties concerned, with corresponding modes of mutual interpretation that are themselves a part of the framework of everyday interactions. In *Au Bonheur*, in keeping with the expansion of everything in the grand store, the clientele is both massed together as an ecstatic female crowd, and also precisely classified into a set of likely psychological types, each exemplified by those named characters first encountered in the drawing room of Mme Desforges. Their typical shopping behaviour is shown at intervals: the over-spender, the sensible bargain-hunter, the well-to-do shoplifter, and so on. These women are deftly profiled; the new form of store engenders a spectrum of specific new psychological types, as seen both from a would-be external perspective—Zola's, here—and on the ground, by the various interested parties— shop staff, family and friends, the women themselves—who all develop their own ways of talking about these typical customer pathologies.

In the department store the behaviours may be more extreme, but a differentiation of customer orientations occurs at all retail levels. *L'Assommoir* reports that general verdict of unspecified neighbouring shopkeepers that Gervaise is a decent sort of customer: 'really, there weren't a whole lot of customers that were as good as she was, paying straight down, not nit-picking, not moaners'. Not a whole lot as good as she was: the phrase evokes both a mode of casual classification and a type of bonding neighbourly chat, with its own conventions of profiling. This is how shopworkers talk about their customers, with the categories for placing them. Calling Gervaise a 'good' customer is a question of specified attributes, like three ticked boxes: prompt payer; not a haggler; not a complainer.

One last, exceptional customer in this regard is worth considering. *Le Ventre de Paris* has an otherwise unoccupied elderly *cliente* who spends her time (but not her money) going in and out of the shops, to gather gossip:

> Throughout the day she would be out and about with her empty basket, on the pretext of having shopping to do, buying nothing, trading bits of news, keeping herself informed of the smallest facts, and so managing to find space in her head for the complete history of the neighbourhood—the buildings, the different floors, and the people. ... She became ill if some unforeseen gap in her notes appeared.[37]

The woman even keeps a sort of mental filing system, and suffers physically if it is incomplete. And perhaps there is something familiar about this zealously comprehensive observer. Zola may have worked with a larger canvas, a more extensive street map, than the locale he shares with this Mlle Saget for the duration of the novel; but in many ways they do the same job, detailing and retailing the latest information, storing it all up for later use. No transaction too big or too small. New lines added every day.

# 3

# ENDINGS
# PLOTS
# EXILE IN ENGLAND

## The Dreyfus affair and beyond

'Soon, all these things will be of only historical interest': 'Bientôt, toutes ces choses n'auront plus qu'un intérêt historique.' These are the words that Zola writes to his wife Alexandrine in November 1899; perhaps pleased with the phrase (and the thought), he repeats it in another letter a few days later: 'all that, let me say it again, will soon be of only historical interest'.[1] What he means is that before too long, the continuing obligations and distractions of the Dreyfus affair, whose main drama was largely done by this time, will be in the past. It will have ceased to press in upon their daily life.

But *only* historical interest? More than a century on, the Dreyfus affair continues to echo and resound with all the fervour of actuality. Far from having quietly passed away into a placidly dormant past, those events of the 1890s surrounding the wrongful incarceration of a Jewish army officer are vividly present still as part of ongoing issues of antisemitism and justice. Renderings and interpretations of it appear in every kind of medium, new and old, from history books and biographies to documentaries, podcasts, and movies—for instance, in Roman Polanski's film of 2019, *An Officer and a Spy*, based on Robert Harris's novel of the same name.[2]

But as Zola's wishful reassurance suggests in a different way, 'history' is not always—and not only—a matter of what is publicly notable or what can be told, and retold, in a clearly developing narrative with its major events and its heroes and villains. In 1899 he trusts that the large public drama of Dreyfus will fade away into a history that no longer impinges on what will by then have become, once again, the peaceful routines of the present. There is also this different history that lies in the small things of private lives, the eventless habits and norms of the everyday that the bigger, more visible histories may threaten or enliven. This kind of history may well disappear once past—and may well, in its ordinariness, be unremarked until it is seen to have changed—with different surrounding conventions and norms, or different surrounding material objects. This is the stuff that surfaces in surviving journals and letters; it is the material of the domestic and working milieux that began, in the nineteenth century, to have a place in the novel, and then gained a more factual foothold in twentieth-century social history. It is the stuff of Zola's own novels about the details of ordinary lives in the modern world.

In Zola's case, as it happens, we have not only the driving force of the Dreyfus case with its drama and plots and with all the documentation and interpretation of that, both then and since. There is also a remarkable archive of the letters he wrote to the two women in his life (at this later point), his wife Alexandrine and Jeanne Rozerot, the mother of his children—letters that mostly exist only because of the separation from them both that was occasioned by the Dreyfus affair itself. These letters, amounting to many hundreds of printed pages, have only been published in the present century—those to Jeanne in 2004 and those to Alexandrine ten years later. They represent a new part of the story, as well as a fascinating new trove of Zola's published writing.

The famous Affair had its beginnings in 1894, in the wake of the verdict of treason passed on Captain Alfred Dreyfus. He was falsely accused of passing documents to the Germans, France's enemy at the time, all the more in the wake of the brutal Franco-Prussian War of 1870; the evidence came down to a memo or *bordereau* supposed to be written in Dreyfus's hand. In a military hearing behind closed doors in December 1894, Dreyfus was found guilty. In early January he was publicly stripped of his honours before being exiled for life to a remote Pacific island, where he arrived the following year.

A turning point in the protracted campaign to reverse the verdict came after Georges Picquart, a high-ranking young officer, realized that the author of the incriminating note, the *bordereau*, was not Dreyfus but another officer called Esterhazy. In the subsequent course of events, Zola's role as a polemical writer was pivotal. In January 1899 came *J'Accuse!*, the famous newspaper article written as an open letter to the president of the Republic, in which Zola denounced the miscarriage of justice, laying out point by point all the facts and evidence. The persuasive force of this piece derived in part from its appearance on the front page of a newspaper, a spectacular intervention. It was itself headline news across the world, an impact inseparable from Zola's status by this time as a household name. This was not his first contribution to the campaign, but it is the one that made history, as it was designed to do. It was sensational.[3]

Following the article, and not unexpectedly, Zola was charged with libel (*diffamation*) and found guilty. Some months later, in July, at the point when it became clear that the appeal against this conviction was about to fail, he fled to England to avoid going to prison—taking the overnight boat train from the Gare du Nord in Paris. For almost a year he was then in exile—the word that he used himself. He spent an initial period in Surrey, first in a hotel near Weybridge and then in two short-term rented houses not far from there; but for most of the time—from the middle of October until his return to France in early June 1899—he lived at the Queen's Hotel in Upper Norwood, in south London, near the then still standing Crystal Palace.

Thanks to the letters to Jeanne and Alexandrine, information about Zola's daily existence over the following months is fuller than for any other period of his life. There was also a journal, kept mainly during the very first weeks, which he called *Pages d'exil*, as well as a book called *Zola in England* by his translator Ernest Vizetelly, who had assisted with the practicalities of the various moves from one place to another. Gauging his market, Vizetelly peppers the narrative with insider anecdotes about the great man abroad—about how, for instance, on his first day, arriving with no change of clothes, he resorted to using sign language at a men's outfitters on Buckingham Palace Road in order to buy himself a shirt, a collar, and socks.[4] Likewise, the *Pages d'exil* include Zola's impressions of everyday cultural differences: in rural Surrey, for instance, he was fascinated to observe English women passing his window on bicycles to do their daily shopping and wearing skirts rather than (as they would in France) culottes.[5]

But it is the voluminous letters, above all, that provide the material for the striking juxtaposition, over this period, of different sides of what is in some sense the same history. On one side there is Zola the international celebrity, famous novelist, leading actor in the much mediatized events of the Dreyfus case, and hence the subject of worldwide speculation in the days that followed his disappearance from Paris. *Where is Zola?* asked all the newspaper headlines, as Vizetelly reports (one hypothesis was Norway; another Switzerland).[6] On the other side there is Zola the private individual, living for many months on his own—incognito, even—and getting on as best he can within the confines of that situation. One side of this history is full of plots and events and the question of how and when it is all going to end. The other side is characterized, most of all, by repetition: each day like the next and the one before.

## Working, living

It has sometimes been suggested that Zola's intervention in the Dreyfus affair enabled him to move beyond the desk-work of a man who 'merely' wrote.[7] In his later years, so this story goes, Zola comes out of his study to play a heroic part in an event of burning national significance—and one that continues to reverberate as a nodal moment in the history of opposition to antisemitism. But Zola had always been an engaged journalist as well as an author of novels, while many of the novels themselves were, or came to be seen as, polemical contributions to social debates.

The journalism typically took the form of sharply argued opinion pieces. Throughout Zola's working life he had written regular columns about contemporary politics—sharp, well informed, often satirical. He had been a journalist before he was a novelist; his training was in writing with a purpose and with clarity. Ultimately, he believed, it was writers who made a difference: 'I mean that the only real and lasting action is to be found in written thought.'[8]

As regards the private Zola, his twofold family life was of relatively recent date. He had been with his wife, Alexandrine, since his twenties; they were married in 1870, and they had no children. In 1888 Zola had fallen in love with Jeanne Rozerot, who was working for Alexandrine in the house. After they had begun a relationship, he set her up in an apartment elsewhere; Alexandrine knew only that Jeanne had left her job. A first child, Denise, was born in 1889, and then a son, Jacques, two years later. Not previously a father, Zola was immensely happy to become one. Shortly after the birth of Jacques, Alexandrine found out. After a period of painful turbulence, the marriage went on, and Alexandrine continued to be the honoured and beloved wife. She was at Zola's side, for instance, when he came to London for several days in 1893, to great acclaim and media attention, invited as a guest of honour by the Institute of Journalists.

With Zola's encouragement, Alexandrine also began to venture out independently—with long autumn stays in Italy on her own in the three years before the exile period of 1898-9. During these absences of hers, in the same way as during his own in England, Zola wrote to her, at length, all the time; the practical fact of the various separations gives rise to the extraordinary archive that the letters now are. It is clear from what is said there and elsewhere that she had begun, quite soon after learning of their existence, to have a role in the children's lives. From time to time they would be brought to visit her; she took them out, she bought presents for them. After Zola's death in 1902 it was Alexandrine who made it possible for Denise and Jacques to be given their father's name; their surname was legally changed to Émile-Zola.

This story—or history—is impossible to recount in a simple way, given the different perspectives, and especially given the weight of all that is unknown and unrecorded. That is true of any biography, or group biography; but in this case it gains added pertinence and piquancy from the significant expansion of the available evidence in recent decades. First of all, from the research of Evelyne Bloch-Dano, whose book *Madame Zola* was published in 1997, it emerged that before she met Zola, Alexandrine had had a baby.[9] That baby was given up for fostering to the Enfants trouvés, a charitable organization that had its origins in the rescue of infant foundlings. It is known that that child died soon after; many did. It is known too that Zola knew about it, since it was he and Alexandrine together who sought out the information about what had become of her child. With this history of both a lost motherhood and a demonstrated fertility, Alexandrine's later childlessness becomes all the more poignant. This hitherto hidden event must have been of utmost importance, whether spoken or not, in the history of the Zolas' marriage, both before and after the birth of Zola's children with Jeanne.

Further reorientations occur through the detail of Zola's letters to the two women. These had been carefully kept by Jacques Émile-Zola, the son of Zola and Jeanne.[10] At the end of his life, he passed them on to his granddaughter, Brigitte Émile-Zola, with the instruction that they should not be published until the present century; she recounts the scene at the start of the second of the books they became, at length, in 2014.[11] The availability of both sets of letters now, thanks to the work of Alain Pagès together with Émile-Zola herself, offers a remarkable picture of the day-by-day doings and emotions of the three people concerned. This is social and personal history at its finest and most moving. It is also, in the twenty-first century, a new extension of Zola's life and lives: still continuing.

The details of daily life in the letters are fulsome and factual; they are everything that is associated with the attentiveness of nineteenth-century domestic realism. But at the same time, the multiple perspectives and the intensely emotional charge of the situation between the three protagonists is more in the style of a twentieth-century modernist scenario. Perhaps, after all, this might have been the ultimate 'experimental novel'—to adapt Zola's own phrase. Take three characters, two intersecting couples, two women, one man, with one relationship public and one clandestine. They have established a provisional *modus vivendi* which is to be tested by a forced geographical separation. Make the separation itself the result of a complicated and still unfolding sequence of dramatic events, and put the now isolated figure not just somewhere else but in a wholly unfamiliar setting, another country. That situation then offers every narrative justification for the description of the milieu. Because the protagonist is a foreigner, it is unimpeachably plausible or *vraisemblable* that that would have to happen. There is a logical reason for him to notice and describe it, which is that he does not know the place or the customs himself, and nor do his addressees.

In a novel there would be multiple angles from which to look at this three-cornered situation. But despite Zola's favoured references to the laboratory or the dissecting table, in practice the writer, unlike the scientist, can only speculate, without any provable or disprovable result. But they *can* speculate. And this, it seems to me, is what Zola may have been mooting, whether intentionally or not, when, decades before the events of the 1890s, in the *Préface* to its second edition, he had first produced his retrospective justification of the plot of *Thérèse Raquin* as being based on some sort of scientific experiment: to see what would happen, given certain character types and certain conditions. The set-up of that novel is itself a triangular situation—two couples and three characters, one woman and two men. So were the plots of the other two early novels, *Madeleine Férat* and *La Confession de Claude*—one with an earlier lover, thought dead, who returns after all, and the other with a still present rival across the way. Two men, one woman, in each of those three cases.

Comparably complex triads had formed the domestic basis of Zola's own life from the very beginning. In his early life, after his father's death, he had lived with two women of different generations, his mother and grandmother. Later, grown up, with Alexandrine and his mother, there was a second iteration of this form. Zola's mother died in 1880, and the relationship with Jeanne Rozerot, much younger than Alexandrine, began eight years later. This was then the third trio in Zola's life to consist of two women loving one man who loves them both.

Zola was well aware of the novelistic qualities of the events he was living through—those of the public sphere, at any rate. (Ironically, he was disparaging about the ubiquitousness of the novel of adultery in French literature, and had said so in a recent article, to which we shall return.) Towards the end of the letters from England to both Alexandrine and Jeanne, the word *dénouement* is used repeatedly to point out the as if aesthetic completion to what has been going on. When, and only when, there is some kind of closure for the Dreyfus process will Zola return to Paris. He is determined not to risk confusing or even impeding that outcome by ending his exile too early. There is also a question, raised as such, of how his return will play out on the stage of its reporting in the media. He often uses the word 'triumph' to speak of the hoped-for collective victory of the Dreyfusards. But he does not himself want to be seen in the starring role of the homecoming hero. In the event, he did slip back unobtrusively, just as (for different reasons) he had departed in haste and in secret. This second time, the journey and the secrecy were planned in meticulous detail, all written out as instructions and plans—for both Jeanne and Alexandrine.

The *dénouement* is not only that of the end of the Dreyfus drama and thereby Zola's return from exile. It is also the end of the novel that he was writing in England for almost the whole time he had been away. The name of that novel is *Fécondité—Fertility*. It is all about the joy of having babies (and the iniquity of not), and it took him—beginning in August and ending in May—nine and a half months to write, a long gestation for a book that came out at a more than healthy 750 pages. The repeated extensions of the stay in England had been a source of frustration all along to Zola, not least because the uncertainty made it difficult to decide when and if Alexandrine and Jeanne (and the children) should visit. But in the final weeks, and especially after he has himself noted the likely confluence of the two completions, Zola starts to enjoy the convenience and satisfaction of the coincidence. The end is in sight, a spot-on simultaneous double delivery and double *dénouement*. It is every author's plotting dream, perhaps—but also, since Zola was inside the two stories still going on in real life, the writing and the exile, it is a double source of tension until the very end. To Alexandrine, in the middle of May 1899:

> At the moment, if I'm still so anxious, it's because in addition to the fever of the last pages there is the fever I'm in with waiting for the resolution of the Affair. You know I have never been able to finish a book without it making me ill.[12]

And at the end of the same letter: 'Is this really at last the approach of the *dénouement*?'[13]

## The consolations of daily life

Before turning to *Fécondité*—the novel itself, aside from its writing—let us pause to consider the continuing, storyless features of Zola's English life, the repeated daily patterns of his solitary existence. The writing of the letters, with their copious detail, itself helps to consolidate the supportive and predictable living conditions that they describe; and as an activity it also has its own place at the end of the day. All through the correspondence with both women Zola talks about his routines in a known and well-ordered domestic space—and talks as well about the fact that he talks about it so much. To Jeanne:

> Sometimes I work a bit too hard, that's all. But I would be so happy to go home with my novel almost finished! I am halfway through, so you can see what a job I still have. I've already described my life so many times that I don't talk about it any more, since it's always

> the same and I would only be repeating myself. All the days are like one another, the only distractions I have are the letters and newspapers that come to me from France. And that will continue, without any change, until the day I go back to you.[14]

Or in outline:

> You know my life, work in the morning, a walk in the afternoon, reading the papers in the evening, and early to bed. I go for weeks without seeing a living soul and without opening my mouth.[15]

There is surely some exaggeration in the second sentence, unless what is meant is that days without any conversation can soon come to feel like forever. But at other times, the silent existence is represented as an appealing element of the enforced retreat; solitude is enabling rather than detrimental to Zola's peace of mind and his ability to maintain a stable pattern of work in a room of his own. With him lacking English and them lacking French, there is no verbal communication with the hotel staff. But he remarks more than once on how they have come to understand his wants and his ways, and he is grateful for their discretion (if they know who it is they are looking after, they never let on).

Some weeks before the quick summary there was a full elaboration of the routine, this time with specified hours, soon after the move to the Queen's Hotel:

> I don't have any major news to give you, for the good reason that nothing happens around me and I live in absolute solitude. I'm just fine in my new place.... My hours have stayed the same, I get up at eight, I have a good wash, I'm brought my *café au lait* at nine, and I read my foreign newspapers; then, I work till lunch, at one; afterwards I make myself go out for an hour or two, with long rambles, until four; at half past four tea is brought to me, and this is

generally when the post from Paris reaches me; then, I immerse myself in the papers until seven; I have dinner; I read some more; and I go to bed around ten. The next day, I start again, always the same thing. So when you are thinking of me you will be able, at any hour of the day, to know precisely what I'm doing. It is all as regular as a clock, and I'm not complaining, because luckily I am never bored.[16]

Not being bored is something like a matter of principle with Zola; it is part of his sense of identity. On one occasion he is annoyed to hear (in a letter from Alexandrine) that his publisher Eugène Fasquelle has told someone else that that's how Zola is at the moment. No, he says. 'I am never bored': the same words.[17] He both depends on and actively enjoys the clock-like continuities of his hours and days.

Work—*travail*—is the fundamental item of the daily agenda, as it had been throughout Zola's life; it is always in the morning, and measured (when a novel is in progress) by the production of several handwritten pages per day.[18] Right after the detailed description to Jeanne of the daily hours, the next paragraph of the letter begins: 'I have got back to my novel in earnest' (it had been broken off for the family's visit). He goes on: 'it is work that sustains me and enables me to accept my solitude bravely'.[19] The quantified daily exercise was a kind of ritual, providing the security and renewal of an assured routine: each day, as he says, like each other day. Over and over again in the letters Zola speaks of this daily work as his *consolation*. It is a constant throughout his life; but in the current predicament it also makes up for the separation from loved ones, and for the stress and perpetual uncertainty of the process of the Affair. It sustained—and comforted—him in the face of all disturbance, both private and public.

In February 1899, during a bleakly anxious period of the Dreyfus events, another letter to Jeanne brings out the vital importance of the writing project as an anchor in the midst of uncertainty:

> It is impossible to know what will happen tomorrow. I have just received a very dark letter from [Octave] Mirbeau who, it is true, usually does think all is lost. We are going through such a crisis that the worst things become possible. Let's wait, and let's count just on ourselves, let's be ready in advance to adjust to all possible eventualities.
>
> The day after tomorrow I'm expecting Fasquelle who will bring me news, if the storm doesn't prevent him from coming: for two days now there have been violent gales once again. Also, the news that is brought to me is just one day's news; and the next day, everything turns out to have changed. Where are we going? I can't hide from you that I have no idea, and that sometimes I wish I had the courage to take you all [Jeanne and the children] to Italy, without more delay, so as at least to live there peacefully.
>
> Happily I am well. This morning I finished the twenty-third chapter of my novel, out of thirty. So that makes just two thirds. I need over two months more to complete the work. I won't be writing the last lines before the end of May. And where will I be?[20]

Like the stormy weather, which may or may not enable a cross-Channel journey to happen, the future is unpredictable from day to day—and fearful: 'the worst things become possible'. In this context the feasible job of work in the form of the current writing project takes on an even greater importance than it had always held for Zola. As he passively waits for news, and waits for the worst, it is the one aspect of his life that can be controlled, both as part of each day and as a long-term prospect and product.

Unlike the indeterminacy of the period of exile, it is manageable and quantifiable and notable as such: one chapter at a time, with an end in sight. After a paragraph wondering whether, after all, and despite the practical difficulties, he should have kept them in England—'we would have managed to work it out'—he signs off with kisses and hugs all round; 'I have just one consolation, telling myself that whatever happens, we will soon be back together again.'[21]

Each day's work, then, as well as providing the comfort of regularity, was also an addition: more lines each day, leading up to the finished text. 'No day without a line': not just a quotidian exercise but a long-term process of accumulation. This too is a kind of consolation. It is part of a finite production: the current project, drafted day by day and page by page and line by line. Away from the uncertainties of the events of the Dreyfus affair, this labour will surely come to a (happy) end, in the form of the completion of the current project. In this second, productive aspect the work eventually departs from the stable space of the daily domestic routine, becoming an object of public appraisal and a contribution to its author's œuvre.

An author like Zola was in one way comparable to a twenty-first-century digital nomad. He could do his job anywhere, given some minimal equipment. As Virginia Woolf would point out in one of the more practical observations of her polemical essay 'Professions for Women', in 1931, paid writing is work that can be done from home, with negligible expenditure on the tools of your trade. All you need is pen and paper, plus in due course a stamp and an envelope to post off the manuscript to a publisher. This is why, she says, writing has been one of the few ways that women, confined to the home, could earn money.[22] To which we may add: it is also why it is the ideal job for a man who is suddenly thrust into isolation: living in a foreign country, cut off from friends and family and not even speaking the local language (he did, for a while, try to learn). He can just get on with it. And it gives him, on any given day, something to do.[23]

To Woolf's emphasis on the cheap materials and flexible location of authorship can be added a further aspect, which is the modernity of this conception of the writer as a worker, paid by the line or the word-count, if not by the hour. Such a mode of regular production often carried over into the distinctive format of first publication, too, via newspaper serialization. A story unfolded day by day, with a point of suspense required at the end of each instalment: high drama, not repetition. This *feuilleton* form was how many of Zola's novels first appeared before subsequently coming out as stand-alone books; like the fixed-time TV serials of the later part of the twentieth century, the instalment format created a climate of anticipation for readers in the real world in which they were published, as new developments of the fiction were eagerly awaited. Zola was adept at exploiting the potential of this system of two-phase publication—the *feuilleton* followed by the full book—and thus of additional income. And by the time of *Fécondité*, when he was read all over the world, this practice of pre-book newspaper serialization occurred with foreign editions too. Long passages of the letters to Alexandrine are taken up with minute instructions for precisely how and to whom the proofs of the still unfinished novel are to be packaged and forwarded from Paris so as to enable translators, most of whom Zola knows from previous assignments, to get on with their job at speed.

During the exile there are other occupations, too, which are mentioned here and there in the letters. Photography, in particular, is a hobby that Zola shares with Alexandrine and is beginning to share with Jeanne. As well as taking pictures himself, he also gives loving attention to the collecting of photographic souvenirs and pictures of his family. He writes in detail, for instance, about seeking a double frame in which to put two small portraits of the children, and has his eye on one he has seen on his walks, in the window of a local photographer's. The best kind of holiday souvenir, he says to Alexandrine when she is away in Italy and wondering what to buy as a present for him or the children, is a useful thing that you come across every day in the ordinary course of things. In the same way photographs can be cherished objects in themselves, as well as reminders of times and places.

Zola is also himself taking pictures of the daily life of the neighbourhoods where he finds himself living. Writing to Jeanne, in October, after the month when she and the children had come over to stay with him in Surrey:

> Yesterday, as the sun was out, I took a few photographs, to complete my collection of the places where I will have lived here. I still haven't got back the ones I took in for developing; I'm really worried they may have spoiled them.—You have no idea how the places where we lived here together awaken at moments in my memory. I see us here or there, on bicycles, or with the children, and the smallest details come back to me. Those are very sweet memories, despite the moments of sadness that we went through.[24]

This passage puts together the sense of photography as the making of a useful record—the various places that, in the future, will have been where he lived in England—with something like the reinvention of memory itself as a kind of photographic mechanism, bringing back 'moments' from the past in all their 'details'. Zola took photographs of local scenes such as the shops and signs and awnings along the main streets in Upper Norwood; or the policeman striding across a road; or the woman wheeling her bike along the path in front of the hotel. These are not only fine photographs in themselves but they are quite exceptional, for this time, as records of the everyday look of a suburban street—not a likely choice of photographic subject. And the photographer was, of all people, Émile Zola—world-famous author. But an author well known for his radically modern depiction, in a much older medium, of otherwise unrepresented places and people.[25]

## Antenatal, anti-anti-natal: *Fécondité*

*Fécondité*, the book written in England, was the first of Zola's final novel series, unmodestly entitled *Les Quatre Évangiles—The Four Gospels* (the last had yet to be written at the time of his death in 1902). Like all his fictions, *Fécondité* was planned out in detail in advance; just as the end of the exile turned out to coincide with the completion of its writing, so it had happened, by great good luck, that he had been just about to begin it when he suddenly had to leave home. Once arrived in England, all he needed was for his useful friend Fernand Desmoulin to bring over some books and the precious documents of the plan, and within a couple of weeks, on 4 August 1898, the work was duly begun.[26] Even during the short hiatus of the first days in England, and even after the tumult of the events that preceded them, he was longing to get down to work again. He needed and thrived on the daily output of lines.

It is not hard to imagine how Zola's newfound fulfilment as a father might have lent itself to the themes of *Fécondité*, which is explicitly a promotion of parenthood. The personal background, not publicly known at the time, is now a compelling underlying dimension to the line Zola takes. Bearing in mind what had been happening in his own life, *Fécondité* cannot but be read as a heartfelt expression of personal belief—if not a grandiose expansion of paternal pride to encompass the whole wide world. But this background is not a missing link to account for an otherwise unlikely choice of theme. Reproduction was a major topic of argument and even activism in the 1890s, in response to a declining birthrate in France and the sense that that was a national problem for which policy solutions should be sought. It is this public context which has generally been seen as the primary spur to the theme of Zola's novel, and it would be a sufficient explanation on its own. There was any amount of talk, and any number of novels, even, about the politics of reproduction.

*Fécondité* narrates the blissful annual baby-making, over many years, of a contented couple who have settled in an idyllic rural location outside Paris—not unlike Médan, where Zola and Alexandrine had built their country house but had had no children.[27] In the course of the novel Marianne and Mathieu Froment have many, many offspring, who almost all (one son becomes a priest) go on to marry and multiply in their turn. One goes off to Africa, where a supplementary Froment base is formed. Years later, in the novel's finale, a young representative of this further family returns to deliver a kind of after-dinner talk about the great Froment future that awaits out there.

With its marking of time via annual births and regular gatherings of the ever-increasing clan, the steady progressions of *Fécondité* are well suited to Zola's episodic style of narration. This mode is one of continuities and seasonal regularities but it is not—far from it—without contrast or tension. For the virtuous happiness of the primary family, ever reproducing their love and harmony, is shadowed all along by an accumulation of viciously contrasting situations. These function as exposés of bad sex, and bad—meaning thwarted—reproduction. Only by means of the constant counter-examples, often presented with the shocking details of an undercover investigation, do the tableaux of parental love and contentment show up in all their self-congratulatory glory. The lurid catalogue of the non-parental includes back-street abortion clinics and maternity homes; neglectful wet-nursing and child-minding; and a host of other businesses providing natal services of every kind—before, during, and after a birth. Most of them are shown as taking advantage of the vulnerabilities of potential or actual parents, desperately seeking, at either extreme, to have or to not have babies.[28]

Many of these various parental or anti-parental practices have their counterparts in present-day cultures, but there is one whose negative representation now seems quite out of place. Astonishingly for a modern reader, Zola's sinister anti-natal world includes middle-class married couples who use contraception, either from the outset, or (just as reprehensible for Zola) when they are already parents. Sometimes his characters speak euphemistically of their *précautions* or *prudence* (the latter being a term much in use in discussions of birth limitation at the time). But the word Zola most often uses is non-technical and judgemental: *la fraude*. To prevent conception is a form of deception or trickery, evading a natural process. Contraception was associated at this time with middle-class privilege and in the novel often (not exclusively) with those who seek out forms of freakish (that is, non-reproductive) sexual behaviour. In two of Zola's exemplary cases, *la fraude* may have been the cause of a couple's infertility (*impuissance*).

Cast into the same unfruitful darkness are those who refrain from sex altogether because of their cold unresponsiveness or refusal, what Zola calls *froideur*. That word—plain 'coldness' in French—would go on to have a long twentieth-century diagnostic use in the form of female 'frigidity'. But both *froideur* and *impuissance* are used by Zola to indicate forms of sexual malfunction which may be thought of as not only wrong but voluntary. To refuse the warmth of sexual union uncomplicated by anti-natural devices is a fault, in Zola's book. Couples who do so are selfish; in their pursuit of no more than their own individual sexual fulfilment, 'la jouissance égoïste', they are turning marital sex into prostitution, complete with all its imagined artifice and excesses.[29] The novel's opening episode tells of Mathieu Froment's late-night resistance to the insistent advances of Sérafine, the frantically over-sexual upper-class woman with whom he had had a torrid affair before his marriage to the lovely maternal Marianne. The rejection finally achieved, he takes the last train back out into the country and into the safely welcoming arms of the waiting wife. Naturally, a new baby—their fifth—is conceived in the snug small hours of that very night.

I have found it difficult to summarize the stance of *Fertilité* without a tone of some incredulity, as if to make sure that I won't be misunderstood as endorsing attitudes on Zola's part that today seem as perverse as he found the behaviours that he condemns. For many decades now it has been the norm in most parts of the developed world that the use of contraception is the appropriate and responsible behaviour for—in the language of our time—sexually active heterosexual adults of reproductive age (who are not presently seeking to have children). The other side of that view is that sexual pleasure can be enjoyed for its own sake—that is, without fear of pregnancy, thanks to the relatively simple and effective methods of contraception that came into use over the course of the twentieth century, the oral 'pill' above all. Freud's *Three Essays on the Theory of Sexuality*, which was published just a few years after *Fécondité*, endorsed in theory that separation of sexuality from reproduction that widely available contraception would bring about in practice.[30] Early advocates of birth control stressed its primary value as making possible the enjoyment of sex for married couples without the perpetual worry about engendering (more) children. That notion of 'family planning' (or, in the US, 'planned parenthood') became the standard phrase in English (and in the Protestant or secular Western countries where it was used) for responsible sexual behaviour.

The novel's hostility to contraception might be seen as surprising given Zola's broadly negative attitude to the Catholic church, which had been at the centre of *Lourdes* (1894) and *Rome* (1896), two of the monumental novels completed in the years before *Fécondité*. But in the 1890s the movement against contraception did not yet carry the Catholic associations it acquired in the course of the twentieth century. The eccentricity and seeming extremity of some of Zola's attitudes is awkward now, in the light of changed assumptions and practices in relation to both contraception and sexuality. We want the writers we love to have been on the right side of history. But the very peculiarity of the case, as it seems today, may show us something about the very different groupings of ideas at that time from those we take for granted today.

Zola's interest in issues of fertility was not restricted to individual choices and practices. In 1896 he had published an article on the problem of 'depopulation'. In the short term the piece had been prompted by the founding of a pro-natalist organization; Zola supports its aim of increasing the French population but thinks that the means it proposes are misguided. You don't, he argues, increase the birthrate by fiscal measures to ease the cost of living for hardworking families. What is needed, instead, is positive images of parenthood; but there are none to be found. This is the context in which, as mentioned above, he complains that the plots of novels are exclusively about adultery, 'l'éternel adultère'—without a baby in sight.[31] Schopenhauer and Wagner, much in the cultural air, don't do the cause any favours either: negativity in the first case, desperate love in the second—and again, no babies. As for the symbolists and the decadents with their girlish youths and boy-bodied women—well, no wonder the birthrate is plummeting! What is needed, instead, is works that will make large families seem attractive. And I have been thinking for years of writing one myself! he says at the start of the piece. *Fécondité*, the novel he did get down to, two years later, would be just that: an extended advertisement for big-time, big-family baby-making.

In the 1890s a rejection of contraception must be set in the context of this widespread public argument about a declining birthrate, and how to remedy it. But Zola's objections should also be seen in a further unexpected connection. Another activist organization founded in 1896 was the Ligue pour la Régénération humaine (League for Human Regeneration); this one was dedicated to the reduction rather than the raising of the birthrate, in the name of the 'neo-Malthusian' thinking which would later be called eugenics (that term was imported from English, and the French movement was strongly influenced by British developments).[32] Today, it is taken for granted that the turn-of-the-century eugenics movement was headed in dangerous directions, and the default condemnation of eugenics is the mirror image of the obvious acceptance of contraception. But in the 1890s and early 1900s those two were commonly associated as a natural pairing. Contraception is a technology for the scientific limitation of human reproduction, which is exactly what eugenics promotes. From this point of view, then, Zola's opposition to contraception would align him with the repudiation of eugenics. And it is striking that *Fécondité*, for all its oddities, makes no distinctions of class or race in its indiscriminate advocacy of natural parenthood. All birth is welcome and wonderful.

But again, it is not a matter of deciding one way or the other: was Zola right or wrong? Should our own views of contraception or eugenics be corrected, or on the other hand must we stop reading him because he had such unacceptable views? The point is rather that there can be no straightforward evaluation of a historical constellation of ideas from the point of a later stage of their evolution—with a different ideological milieu of contestation and consensus. What is valuable, instead, is to see with what different connections and cultural associations an idea that we think we know can be advocated or challenged at an earlier moment of its history.

Many features of *Fécondité*'s presentation of the abuses of modern reproductive and contra-reproductive arrangements closely resemble critiques and exposés of the twenty-first-century fertility industry. There is a celebrity obstetrician, for instance, whose experimental operations are reported in the papers. There are clinics and doctors that profit from women prepared to try anything, at any cost, that may give them a chance of having a child of their own; while at the same time, equally active enterprises and individuals exploit women with the opposite desperate need to get rid of a baby. One business, run by a Mme Rouche, caters for both these extremes; she has added to her stillborns speciality with the marketing of a supposedly infallible drug to combat chronic infertility.

On the patient side, there is the roller-coaster experience of a woman who will try anything in the world to get pregnant and who is 'broken by the continual alternation of hope and despair'. This woman is always madly seeking out new medications; she 'scans the newspapers every morning in search of advertisements for a new remedy or the address of some questionable enterprise where they made their profits from infertile mothers in the same way that others made theirs from over-fertile mothers'.[33] There is a case of counter-reproductive tourism in the person of a mysterious English woman called Amy who keeps coming back to give birth one more time (and then give up the child) at the more upmarket of the novel's two featured maternity homes. Amy, who speaks no French, is an object of speculation for fellow regulars: is her not learning the language a strategy, so as not to have to let on what her occupation is? They wonder as well why she never bothers with the postnatal sterilization treatment on offer, which would surely save her from having to take the boat to France so frequently.

In a different vein there are moving vignettes of the impact of childlessness on the private life of a couple—as with the Beauchênes, whose only child has died, and who have been trying without success to conceive another. 'Ils ne fraudaient plus': they were no longer using contraception.[34] At one point the pair of them erupt into furious mutual recriminations about their sex life, which they have never discussed before, in the presence of the family doctor. The wife says that she never refused her husband sex; he says that acceptance can feel like withholding at the same time.[35]

Knowing the outline of Zola's own life in the years before *Fécondité*, the personal resonance of its idealization of parental love and all things procreative seems clear. But there are biographical correspondences to be found in the darker sides of the novel too. Constance Beauchêne asks Mathieu Froment, who is her cousin, to institute a search for the child she knows that her husband fathered some years ago. This Mathieu duly does, having first wondered why she might want this: even if the child were found, this would not give her the new, replacement baby that she longs for. When he probes gently, she says simply, 'I don't know what I'm asking.'[36] He does wonder whether there might be some wish to save the family business 'empire' by acquiring an heir for it, 'beyond her prejudices and bitterness':

> But as yet this was no more than a storm of confused sensations, and all there was in her being was that abandoned torment of the mother who no longer has a child, who will never again have one, who has reached the point of wanting to recover another

woman's child, tortured as she is by the mad fantasy of making it a little bit her own.[37]

This is written by a man who, years before, with his wife, had undertaken the same inquiry that his fictional character Mathieu now makes on Constance's behalf: seeking then to find out what had happened to the baby that Alexandrine, years before *that*, had relinquished for adoption.

There is a further connection for Zola. Now, in the 1890s, his own wife, like Constance, is a childless woman whose husband has had children with someone else. Alexandrine had begun to establish a tentative relationship of her own with Denise and Jacques—who would ultimately, through her initiative after his death, acquire their father's name. The novel hints at the complexities of emotion and connection that are brought together in the extraordinary real story of Alexandrine and Émile's long life as non-parents together despite each of them, separately, having had children of their own.

Constance's desperate plea to Mathieu is preceded, in the same room, by a parallel outpouring of female grief on the part of the novel's representative sex-mad female, Sérafine—the same woman who, unsuccessfully, tried at the start to keep Mathieu from going home to his wife. That was in effect the symbolic choice between sex and babies, and our hero happily made the right call, thereby setting the novel securely on its 750-page generative way. Sérafine now lives with the devastating result of a sterilization operation, which was meant to enhance her sex life by taking away the fear of pregnancy altogether. It has certainly achieved the second of those aims, but it has also done two other things, by causing her body to age dramatically and messing up her sexual functions too. By bringing together these two suffering women, treated by the same practitioner, Zola is able to highlight both the symmetry and the contrast of their thwarted desires. Sérafine is speaking to Mathieu before Constance's arrival:

> 'Oh, that Gaude! Did I tell you that Constance begged me to take her to his clinic, in the hope that he would make it possible for her to have a child? ... That poor Constance, I think she's as unhinged as I am, she's so mad about wanting to replace her Maurice. She's started confiding in me, she tells me extraordinary things, I've never run around Paris more wildly [than she does], even in the times of my worst madness. It must be true, in fact, that this desire to be a mother is as violent and as devastating as the other desire, the great desire, my desire ... And so what! it's still me who suffers more. I'm sure she struggles with despair, she tries everything. But oh, if I were to tell you about the horrible battle I've had, in search of lost pleasure!'[38]

The spectacle of a desperate woman protesting her female fate is a familiar dramatic scenario going back to Greek tragedy. Here the theatrical tone is reinforced by the mention of the other woman as a confidant as well as a fellow sufferer. But behind the familiar façade are new expectations and assumptions. Constance's lament for the loss of motherhood is common enough, but to set it alongside what is represented as a comparable and parallel female complaint about the loss of sexual capacity is radically different. The theoretical separation of sex from reproduction is embodied in two women with opposite inclinations, two equally compelling but utterly different desires, one for motherhood and one for sexual pleasure. And this is the point that Sérafine herself is making, as if to assert a new manifesto for modern female tragedy.

In terms of sexual desire specifically, Sérafine's sexual overdrive casts her at the opposite end of the spectrum from a woman who suffers from an absence of sexual desire. But it is significant that she describes her passions and the loss of them without any reference to men. This has nothing to do with her attractiveness to others; instead, the source of grief is declared to be her own 'lost pleasure'. Beyond the extreme form taken by Sérafine's self-centred urges, a more basic point is that Zola assumes that women, in the same way as men, are subjects of sexual desire. The same equivalence between the sexes is found in the representation of women's infertility. He uses the word *châtrée*—literally, 'castrated'—for a woman whose Fallopian tubes have been tied, thus presenting the operation as directly comparable to male sterilization.

*Fécondité* also presents a detailed exposé of the wet-nursing 'industry' (Zola's word),[39] with its exploitation both of the women who breastfeed other women's babies (at the cost of their own) and of those who are obliged to send their babies away for another woman to nurse so that they can continue to earn a living themselves. The featured character for this situation is Mme Menoux, who works all hours in her small shop and is regularly pressed into paying over the odds to the unscrupulous agent who places babies with foster-mothers. This woman, Mme Couteau, recruits from a village in Normandy where wet-nursing is allegedly the mainstay local industry. It works on a principle of rapid turnover: 'the goods don't spend long in the houses. The faster the circulation, the more that die, the more the profit.'[40] This is why, the informant goes on to explain, this Mme Couteau is so keen to pick up all the newborns she can on her weekly day trips to Paris on the train.

With regard to well-off, non-working women who hire live-in *nourrices* to breastfeed their babies, Zola has no sympathy. But he finds a cleverly light-handed way to make his argument. The scene is an evening event at the Beauchênes', long before the death of their child, Maurice. The voice of reason is that of Dr Boutan:

> 'So it's decided, doctor, you're going to have Parliament pass a law making it obligatory for mothers to breastfeed?'
> 'My God, why not?'
> This gave Beauchêne a topic for gross witticisms, everything that a law like that would turn upside down in the way of habits and customs, and civilized life would be put on hold, the *salons* shut down on account of general breastfeeding, and not a woman left who would still have a presentable bosom beyond the age of thirty, and husbands would be forced to form trade unions, to have a harem where they could get substitute wives when their own were cloistered away with their wet-nursing duties.
> 'So ultimately, you want a revolution.'
> 'A revolution, yes,' said the doctor gently. 'It will happen.'[41]

It is Beauchêne's own mockery that is mocked—and the case for this revolution is made by blowing up the counter-arguments into self-interested absurdity. Wives are for sex, men need sex, and a demanding baby gets in the way of that. In Beauchêne's case, the *serin* or harem is already a partial reality: right before this conversation he has been having a private word with Mathieu to make sure that his newborn non-marital baby, the child of a worker at his factory, was duly handed over for fostering; this is the baby that Constance, many years later, will want Mathieu to find for her.[42]

*Fécondité* moves off at the end into that open future of ever more pregnancies and births, stemming from the Adamic original couple of Mathieu and Marianne, and ultimately pushing beyond the environs of Paris and even of France. That infinitely expansive family prospect felt uncomfortable even to would-be supportive reviewers at the time, like the socialist Charles Péguy, who pointed out that Marianne 'gives birth to a race of bourgeois', while her husband, from modest beginnings, simply becomes a boss or *patron*. Rather than being about humanity and solidarity, this is 'the book of the conquest of humanity by the Froments'.[43] Because of its specific siting in Africa—in a region, moreover, which had just (in June 1898) been the object of a treaty between Britain and France—there is no escaping the colonial implications of this prospect.[44] The natives—'*laboureurs indigènes*'—are mentioned only as lacking in enterprise; they do no work (since harvests are naturally good) and are uninterested in adopting new farming technologies.[45] Still, the mythical aspect of the novel that seems to confine the whole populating project to just one impossibly extending family stops short of stressing a specifically nationalistic or empire-building agenda. Instead, the future horizon is closer to myth. The 'exodus' of the novel's last sentence is biblically patriarchal in its unrolling of endless generations of the paradisical tribe, with room for all.[46]

Zola was uplifted by his own ending to *Fécondité*. Writing to Alexandrine, who had been faithfully acting as a research assistant on his behalf, he tells her one day in May 1899 how the previous night he had been devouring the articles from the Larousse encyclopaedia that she has copied out for him and sent over to England. Her work will enable him, he says, to finish *Fécondité* with a flourish:

> Fasquelle too has sent me some documents I asked him for about Timbuctoo and the Sudan. I spent yesterday, up till midnight in the evening, studying the notes you provided me with yourself, as well as the two books I'd just received; and I am very pleased, that's me fully informed, I have the means of writing a superb piece. That's such a delight, because it gives me the dream *dénouement*, an admirable ending for a novel. It works very well.—At the moment, if I'm still so anxious, it's because the excitement [*fièvre*] of the last pages is added to the excitement of waiting with regard to the resolution of the [Dreyfus] affair. You know that I've never been able to finish a book without it making me ill. So, I hope to be much more calm when I've got rid of the anguish of my book, in the delight of having eventually got it standing up on its two legs. And then I'll have all my energy for welcoming the judgement [about Dreyfus], whatever it turns out to be.[47]

Dream *dénouement* or not for the novel's own story, there could be no doubt of the reality of its completion. After months of the relentlessly regular production of pages, *Fécondité* will come to its definite end and then go forth into the world as an independent being, on its own two metaphorical legs. (It did not do well, despite the 30,000 posters in Paris that announced the first day of its serialization. And almost alone among Zola's many novels, it has never been issued in a cheap paperback edition.)[48]

That ending, as Zola is hoping by now, will itself coincide with the provisional resolution of the Affair, and then his return from exile. This is stated even more directly at the end of the same letter to Alexandrine. The situation has changed even in the course of its writing, with the arrival of the evening post and her latest letter, with more good news about the likely outcome of the ongoing official report: 'It's half past nine, and the post is here at last, bringing me your good letter. It gives me great joy, it reassures me at last.'[49] He says he will digest it properly once he has posted this present letter and come back upstairs again. Then he signs off like this, with the hybrid pet name that they shared (both using it as an endearment for the other):

> Finally, is this really the approach of the *dénouement*? Do we get to be a little bit calm and happy? My poor heart is beating fit to burst. You can't imagine the joy you have just sent your poor dog-wolf-cat, at nearly ten o'clock at night, in this vast dark country where he is alone.[50]

This May letter brings out all the many kinds of ending in play at this stage of Zola's exile: of the writing of the novel, of the story the novel tells, and of the exile in England itself.

## Afterstories

It is the autumn of 1899 and Zola has been back in France for a few months after his time in England. The heat of political tensions has diminished now that Dreyfus, although not yet officially exonerated, has been brought back to France from his remote island imprisonment. Alexandrine has gone off on a holiday of her own to Italy, as she used to do. In that context Zola has resumed his practice of writing long letters to her, almost every other day, in which, according to custom, he reports on his doings—including, sometimes, with the children. There are accounts of who he has met with, what is going on at home, what he's eaten, what so and so said—and there are worries about whether his letters have reached her or whether hers have gone astray, with attendant reflections on the inefficiency of the postal service in Italy: a great many paragraphs, in fact, on these subjects.

In these letters Zola is proud, or mock-proud, to tell Alexandrine about the Thursday soirées that he has hosted on his own at their apartment. At these events she is toasted by their mutual friends, and lovingly honoured in her absence: A bunch of violets is placed on the table where she would have sat. M. Zola buys the flowers himself, and puts a few of them in with the letter afterwards, for her to be able to share in the occasion. But on the evening of Thursday 12 October an incident that is out of the ordinary has occurred which Zola reports in the letter he writes that same night, before going to bed (he almost always writes last thing in this way):

> The evening was really friendly, but a bit uneven [*accidentée*]. Jules [a servant] had initially wanted to light the heater, which had gone out in the evening, and he had to give up on it, as smoke was emerging from all the outlets. So, at that point I wanted to light the fire in my chimney [in his study], and although Jules had lifted the cover, such a quantity of smoke was produced that we had to escape, opening all the windows. In the street people thought there was a fire. We couldn't get back into my study till ten o'clock, for tea. I don't know what could have happened, tomorrow I'll get the chimney man in.[51]

A serious and frightening disruption; but from what he says, only short-term—improbable as that may seem, given the scale of it.

Perhaps Zola is reassuring himself as much as reassuring Alexandrine, who will be getting the news on her own and far away. The study was re-entered, tea was sipped, and tomorrow an expert will come and investigate what the problem was. Everything will soon be back to normal.

It may be all the more important to re-establish a sense of calm because this had been a day of disturbance even before the events of the evening. The smoking chimney comes only right at the end of the letter, in due chronological order following long accounts of two visits earlier on. The first was from Picquart's mistress, 'cette dame Monnier', 'who must be after something', he says; and the other, 'the important and worrying visit', from Percy Spalding and his wife. Spalding worked for Zola's London publishers, Chatto & Windus, and had come to let Zola know that his English translator, Ernest Vizetelly, had embezzled a substantial sum of the firm's money which he had claimed he borrowed for Zola's use at the start of his exile; there was even a forged signature of receipt. This was an explosive matter, not least because of the role Vizetelly had taken on as Zola's personal friend and guide during the time in England.

The evening evacuation comes after all this, in the order of the day and the order of the letter. After that culminating story has been told, there is one more sentence before the letter turns away:

> Desmoulin claims that some anti-Dreyfusards climbed up on the roof and blocked our chimneys.[52]

Reading this for the first time, I must have gasped out loud—I was on a bus, and people turned round to see if something was wrong. It was the same for me when I first came upon the moment in *L'Assommoir* when Coupeau, without any narrative warning, suddenly falls off the roof. But here, at the end of this letter from the final weeks of the nineteenth century, the shock is a different shock. Because you know, as you read it, that what Desmoulin surmises is precisely what really is going to happen, and therefore quite likely what happened this time as well. In three more years—in September 1902—Zola and Alexandrine, just returned from Médan to Paris, would be overcome by fumes from the chimney in their bedroom, and Zola would not survive. Anti-Dreyfusards, very probably, as we know now—but was not known then, was barely investigated then; and more on that in a moment.

To begin with, some other elements of the shock of this story need to be unpicked. The reader's incredulity comes in part, I think, from the fact that the incident reads like something straight out of a novel. It reads, that is, like a carefully planted, *too* carefully planted narrative anticipation: a little bit obvious, in retrospect. Here is this domestic incident in the middle of a party, alarming at the time, but brought under control; the protagonists calm themselves down, drink their tea, and settle down for the night as if nothing much has happened. Everything is once again in order; all is well. But no! For at some later stage, many pages and several years on, the incident will be repeated, this time in a final and fully catastrophic form. The chimney will once more be blocked and this time the hero will die. What Fernand Desmoulin said—in jest? Suspiciously? It isn't clear— will turn out to have been a prophecy as well as a diagnosis. He was right; he was ignored; and the worst then went ahead and happened, after all.

And the person or the character to whom this happens is Émile Zola, the famous Zola, writer of thirty novels all told. Novels whose plots, like no others before or since, are meticulously planned, with every event and movement carefully set up and laid out in advance. There are accidents that happen in the stories recounted—but there are no accidents in the telling, in the faultless enactment, page by page and line by line, of the narrative sequence according to the pre-arranged schema. Like any writer of fiction, moreover, Zola can do whatever he chooses with his plotting. He is free to have a chimney blocked up or a character die or be saved from a fire—blown up or else pulled from the wreckage. Yet the horrors, the triumphs, the rescues, and the murders are always part of a wider purpose. They do not occur in isolation, otherwise they would not be part of a connected story—or a likely story according to the conventions of the day or the genre. But also, quite simply, they do not occur. They are stories—they are 'only' stories. We read them; and no one has died.

Skilled and schematic as he is in his novel-writing, Zola will also drop hints along the way, little tokens of suggestion or warning that may not be obvious at the time, but that readers may retrospectively grasp as having been put there deliberately so as to function later as looking like precursors of subsequent events. In other words, he will set up that proleptic sequence which Desmoulin's fatal remark would have been, had it been in a novel and not on a real Thursday night. The example which comes to mind now, in this context, is from *La Conquête de Plassans* (*The Conquest of Plassans*), a notably under-read novel (historically, it has had the lowest sales of all the Rougon-Macquarts) from early on in the series; it was published in 1874. In this painfully comic story of small-town politics, the previously peaceable home of the Mouret family, two parents and three children, is progressively occupied, to the point of usurpation, by a cast of grotesque lodgers, the cohabitees from hell. The primary loser in this situation is François Mouret, the father and husband, who, treated by others as if he is mad, is sent away to an asylum—where he really does then lose all grasp of his former identity and reality. (This Mouret is the father of the Octave Mouret who will later be the philanderer of *Pot-Bouille* and then the charismatic owner of the department store in *Au Bonheur des Dames*; in the course of the present novel he leaves home for Marseille as a young adult.) One night, eventually, François Mouret escapes from the institution and returns to his house, which he systematically sets alight in a conflagration that causes the death of all four of the evil lodgers.

The description of the minutes that lead up to the start of the fire and then the struggle with two of the lodgers (all the family members are absent) is brilliantly paced—quite literally so, as the returning Mouret, now as if an intruder in his own home, creeps around on all fours, up and down the stairs, and from one room to another. This individual, this being, who has been expelled from his own home and reduced to the crawling condition of an insect, could be an embryonic version of Gregor Samsa in *The Metamorphosis*, which was published a decade or so after Zola's death—in 1915. In the unforgettable opening of that story, Gregor wakes up one morning to find himself, inexplicably, transformed into a tiny and multi-limbed creeping creature.[53]

In both cases, the story and the novel, the bestial abjection of the previously robust man is a sign of how he has lost his status in his own home. For Gregor, the change is sudden—overnight—and physical (he really does have an insect's body now); whereas for

François Mouret, it is the result of a gradual process of deprivation and diminution, the combined effect of all the separate acts and speeches that have made him an object of contempt for all around him. In Kafka's story some comparable changes in the power dynamics of the household do occur, including for a time a trio of peculiar lodgers, but after the transformation, and as a result of it—rather than, as in Mouret's case, before. Another vital difference is that unlike Gregor, the multi-limbed Mouret is not at this point a passive sufferer but is in the act of taking revenge. Methodically making his preparations to set the place alight, 'He seemed to have been endowed with a new life and a logic of movements that were extraordinary.'[54] That *logic* of extraordinary movements beautifully captures a prowess of bodily thinking whose capacities go beyond those that now look like the clumsily upright and uncoordinated human adult.

Up to this point Mouret has been passive in the face of all the indignities visited upon him, even including his eviction from his own home and confinement in a mental hospital. Now he rises to the occasion. The fire has begun. Two of the lodgers sleep on in their drunken torpor, but the other two are on the verge of getting out. One of them, a somnolent priest with the fabulous first name of Ovide, is being hauled downstairs on the shoulders of his indomitable old mother, Mme Faujas. Still calling out for his wife, Marthe, who is nowhere to be found, Mouret tackles the enemy, this man whose mother and sister have been taking over the spaces and the contents of his house, while he, in his clerical capacity, has been taking over the heart and mind of Marthe Mouret. Mouret leaps out at Mme Faujas as she is about to come downstairs with her precious burden; he wrestles with

Ovide, and Ovide dies. He succeeds—at the cost of his own life—in stopping them both from escaping; meanwhile the other pair of invasive lodgers, the Truches, expire in the space of a sentence.

It is worth dwelling for a moment on the force of Mouret's return and revenge. This is a man who has been deprived of his humanity, removed from his home and regarded as having lost his reason. There is no one, any longer, who listens to him or recognizes him for who he is (or rather, now, who he was). Yet, as the final episode shows, he is fully capable of forming an elaborate design and carrying it out—literally carrying the piles of logs to the strategic points for maximum impact when they are set alight.

It only remains, in one final chapter, for the consequences of both the fire at the Mourets' and Marthe's simultaneous heart attack at her parents' house to be dealt with in this novel's customary sampling of the talk of the town. The event is in fact a kind of spectacle for all the neighbours, somewhat as if they are watching it as a theatrical entertainment, or … reading it in a novel. One of them, with a position in local government, has already demanded an official investigation, as he announces with gloriously intricate pomposity: 'I believe that the accident was not without malicious intent.'[55] A young daughter of one of the neighbours, Aurélie, says that she saw who did it—it was M. Mouret. The summary of the discussion that follows is Zola's laconic satire at its best:

> The group of them were commenting on this dreadful occurrence, a homeowner burning his tenants. M. de Bourdeu got worked up over mental hospitals; the surveillance in them was

conducted in a wholly inadequate way. In truth, M. de Bourdeu was trembling at the thought of seeing the prefecture that Father Faujas had promised him go up in flames.

'Mad people are full of resentment,' said M. de Condamin, simply.[56]

In this last part of *La Conquête de Plassans* François Mouret has lost—been deprived of—his local identity as father and citizen; he has been reduced to the status of one who is incapable of looking after himself, and from whom others must be protected—rightly, as then it turns out, with the self-fulfilment of that mad-making logic.

But now let us go back for a moment to a scene that takes place much earlier in the novel. Mouret is with his daughter, Désirée, who is a teenager but needs to be constantly watched. Marthe has gone out, and the situation is described like this:

> Mouret stayed on his own at home with Désirée. These days, he often looked after her. This big child, who was approaching her sixteenth year, could have fallen into the pond or set fire to the house, playing with matches, like a little girl of six.[57]

Read in retrospect, after we know what will happen at the end, this is a poignantly planted comment. For someone will indeed be setting fire to the house; yet it will not be Désirée. Instead it will be the person whose role in this scene is to prevent the possibility of just such an accident. And by the time of the fire—the fire that he sets—Mouret will himself have been returned to something like a state of infantile incapacity. He will have escaped from a situation in which, like his daughter, he is constantly under surveillance. And once again, the layers of that resemblance are further complicated by the comparison and rearrangements of roles. Initially it is the child, later the young woman, who has learning difficulties and needs to be taken care of in ways that are out of the ordinary. But gradually that position will come to be occupied by her father who already, at this earlier time, is beginning to be regarded by his male friends as what they call *touché*—'touched'.[58]

So here is Zola, in a work of fiction, setting up a scene which will figure, later on, as having been an ironic prelude to what really—really in the fiction—does go on to happen. First episode: watch out, the house could be set on fire, take precautions. Second episode: that same house is indeed set on fire, by the same person who was preventing it before. First stage: a person without full mental capacity is the sort of person who might set fire to a house. Second stage: a person deemed to lack full mental capacity sets fire to a house. All that—that story, in the real time of its own publication in the 1870s—may then figure for later readers—readers after the fateful fire of 1902—as a prefiguration of the uncanny, appalling true sequence of first the smoking heater and fireplace of 1899 and then the follow-up, a few years later, when the victim and narrator of that first incident did not live this time to tell the tale. We then become the post-mortem readers of the primary event—the event whose full potential significance was ignored or unknowable at the time.

There is the further parallel to the previous—fictional—sequence in that here, too, a seeming detail of the earlier moment will come to the fore in the second. In the novel, it is mad people and children who set houses on fire—so you have to take care. And then, at the end, a mad person really does do that. In the history of Zola it is anti-Dreyfusards who might be suspected of arson.

And then, at the end, it is almost certainly anti-Dreyfusards who really do—and who probably really did on the previous occasion as well. In the same way, the anticipatory passage, of merely anecdotal interest at the time (because no one acted on Desmoulin's suggestion), then takes on profound significance in the light—in the blaze—of the subsequent disaster.

So the disturbing story of the belated foreshadowing has every appearance of being like a novel—of being contrived, set up as a pair of episodes to create and enhance the reader's sense of a drama. Close at hand is a novel about just such a sequence of speculation about fire that is followed by an actual fire; a novel, moreover, that is written by the very man who, on the second attempt, became the victim of the plot to remove him from his house.

### 'Fire!'

Quoting this cry out loud, you have to be careful that it will be clear that the exclamation is not for real. No other word, no other shout, no matter the speaker or the circumstance, carries so much sudden force—upsetting whatever is going on at the moment, and bringing together those present in some kind of collective response to a threat that affects them all, whether that response is primarily one of panic or purposeful action. So exceptional and so powerful is this situation that knowingly calling out *Fire!* in a crowded theatre is said to have been the one instance of unprotected speech, not covered by the American First Amendment. The question of how and if it ever was, based on a Supreme Court ruling in 1919 by Justice Oliver Wendell

Holmes Jr, is the subject of long threads of online debate. But for our purposes, I want instead to turn to a European contemporary who evoked the crying of *Fire!* in a theatre as a potent analogy for what goes on, routinely, in a highly idiosyncratic modern situation.

Born sixteen years after Zola, in 1856, Freud was another controversial writer of international significance and prodigious output. Both men were known for writing about sex—and both also wrote about just about everything else. By the end of his life Freud had clocked up the twenty-four long volumes of what is now, in English, the Standard Edition: it is a fairly close match to Zola's twenty novels (from the Rougon-Macquart series) and counting. Adjacent as they are in historical time, Zola and Freud are rarely compared either biographically or in any other way. But like Zola, Freud spent a year at the end of his life—the very last year, in his case—in exile in England because of events directly involving antisemitism: Freud left Vienna for London shortly after the Nazi Anschluss, in 1938. And Freud definitely—like most other thinking Europeans of his time—read Zola.

For instance, Freud had read *Fécondité* soon after its publication— at least, in the spring of 1900 he gave a talk on it to his local chapter of the Jewish organization B'nai B'rith. Writing to his friend Wilhelm Fliess the day after this event, he said:

> Yesterday I gave a lecture on Zola's *Fécondité* before my society. I am always ill prepared; actually I start only an hour before—much as one writes a German composition in school. During the night from Monday to Tuesday, I dreamed inordinately of this lecture. I explained that I had to go home to fetch the book, did not find the way, and got lost; the weather was miserable, I made no headway, and during all these delays I worked out part of the talk. The

obstacles, therefore, were only pretexts to gain time for working on it. The brethren, moreover, were unkind and scornful of me—conduct that is apt, quite surely, to reduce my interest in the success of the lecture.[59]

This mode of last-minute anxious dreaming and hasty preparation is something like the reverse of Zola's meticulous planning. Tantalizingly, the notes for the talk (from what Freud says, it can't have been written out!) are lost.

There is a Zolian sequel to Freud's missing lecture, too. In 1907 he was invited to contribute to a round-up of famous people's 'ten good books', and one of his picks was none other than *Fécondité*. (For what it's worth, the others included Rudyard Kipling's *Jungle Book*, Mark Twain's *Sketches*, and Macaulay's *Essays*.)[60] Tempting as it is, though, we should not read too much into *Fécondité*'s seemingly glorious elevation. For one thing, Freud says that he might have chosen any other work by Zola—and gives as an example *Le Docteur Pascal* (*Doctor Pascal*) (1893), the last of the Rougon-Macquarts. He also explains that, in the absence of amplification, he has taken the rubric for the ten good books to mean something less awesome than if the defining adjective had been, say, 'magnificent' (cue for Homer or Shakespeare) or else 'favourite' (he would have said Milton's *Paradise Lost*, for instance). He takes 'good', he says, to mean something like a good read—what you would recommend to a friend.

A few years after this, with the two-person talking therapy of psychoanalysis beginning to become established around the world, Freud wrote a number of short papers for fellow practitioners in the developing new field. He discussed problems and questions to do with the course of a treatment: what he calls the 'technique' of psychoanalysis. One of these papers, 'Observations of Transference-Love', from 1915, tackles an issue not broached before—or not in print—which is the tendency of patients, almost inevitably, to think they have fallen in love with their analyst— and for this then to seem to have taken over from the previous ongoing conversation between patient and therapist, as if that no longer mattered:

> No matter how amenable she has been up till then, she suddenly loses all understanding of the treatment and all interest in it, and will not speak or hear about anything but her love, which she demands to have returned. She gives up her symptoms or pays no attention to them; indeed, she declares that she is well.

What is to be done? These preliminary sentences set up a situation and create some suspense: what is likely to happen next? Then comes the shocking analogy:

> There is a complete change of scene; it is as though some piece of make-believe had been stopped by the sudden irruption of reality—as when, for instance, a cry of fire [*Feuerlärm*] is raised during a theatrical performance. No doctor who experiences this for the first time will find it easy to retain his grasp on the analytic situation and to keep clear of the illusion that the treatment is really at an end.[61]

The comparison has the same effect as the dramatic interruption it evokes: it carries all before it, to the point of reversing the poles of reality and fiction. For it is not the falling in love but rather what was going on before that becomes as it were 'some piece of make-believe', a *Spiel*, and it is the patient's overwhelming passion that is the 'sudden irruption of reality'. And the sentence also seems to confirm the priority of the imaginary reality: 'There is a complete change of scene', Freud says. So we have been at a play all along.

The cry of *Fire!* in a theatre comes in like an offshoot of this initial 'complete change of scene': it is its most extreme illustration. It is also an amplification—the audible shout or scream now on top of the calmer visual shift of the stage-set. However many times it has happened, it is a one-off, a unique experience, the first time it happens to any particular practitioner. Like falling in love itself, as he doesn't quite say. The doctor facing this predicament no longer knows where he is or what's going on in what used to be the steady state of the continuing treatment; it will be hard to hold on, to 'retain his grasp', *festzuhalten*. It will seem as if it is all over, that—like the close of a performance—this is really the end.

But the end of what? If anything is clear from this powerful passage, it is that it is impossible to separate a ground of reality from the scenes or illusions that surround or supplant it. The new illusion or reality that bursts in on the scene will break up all the supports—all the props—that were there up until then. If a theatrical performance is abruptly terminated, that is only the end of an illusion; it was never considered real to begin with. Only the force of the new reality or illusion, whichever and whatever it is, will count.

The rest of Freud's essay twists and turns and twists again in an effort to sort out whether or not the patient's transference love is any different from actual falling in love—or if that, in any case, is really real, whatever real might even be for this strangest of human phenomena. All love borders on the pathological, he says. 'Transference-love has perhaps a degree less of freedom than the love which appears in ordinary life and is called normal; it displays its dependence on the infantile pattern more clearly and is less adaptable and capable of modification; but that is all.'[62]

I think that what Freud describes in this essay, through this conflation of conflagrations, may be at the heart of the shock effect of the first fire, and the reported remark, in the story of Zola's final years. The scandal is because it is better than a story, more than a story. 'Stranger than fiction', in the phrase whose own clichéd familiarity now detracts from the real disturbance of the phenomenon. So also, stranger than stranger than fiction, because the effect is to find that the plotting of a dramatic story has superseded the stable reality of everyday life—whether the sessions of a psychoanalytic treatment or the weekly gatherings of friends. From this point of view it would not really matter whether Desmoulin meant what he said, or thought he was making a joke. It would not even matter whether at this stage or even in 1902 the chimney had really been blocked by anti-Dreyfusards in an attempt to assassinate Zola. What matters is the plotting, as opposed to the putative plot: the sequence of the two events which appear to be linked in retrospect. When you know what the second act was, the first then looks like a rehearsal of it.

The disturbance for the reader is itself twofold. First, in relation to the story: the sequence itself, as a story, appears to be perfectly plotted. It reads, that is, just like a novel, a story by design. And second, in relation to the reality: it could have been stopped! He did die, and here in plain sight or plain words is the warning, long before, that might have prevented it.

This then conjures up a second Freudian parallel, this time with what is known as the dream of the burning child. The dream occurs shortly after the death of a small boy; his father is sleeping in the room adjoining the one where the child's body is laid out, with candles around it, watched over by an old man. In the father's dream, the boy comes to him, telling him that there is a fire: 'Father, don't you see I'm burning?'[63] The father wakes up, goes to the next room, and finds that the old man has fallen asleep, while one of the candles has fallen onto the child's body, burning part of his arm. So there really has been a fire. Freud interprets the dream as embodying the wish that the child be not dead after all, since he comes to raise the alarm himself. If only (going back in time) there had been a warning which could have been heeded; then the boy would still be here. We think of Desmoulin, whose unconsciously warning words, encountered in the too late time of the future, arrive in the same way like an impossible hope, an undoing of what has irrevocably happened.

All this may have conducted us, in an orderly manner, some way away from the undoubted reality of the smoke-filled rooms in the Zolas' apartment on the rue de Bruxelles in October 1899; and then again three years later at the end of September 1902. But if we return now to the earlier of the two incidents, what we find is a swift recuperation. Zola says to Alexandrine that he will be getting the chimney looked at tomorrow by a professional, the *fumiste*; but what the *fumiste* said, if one came, is not reported in any subsequent communication. In any case Zola would not have been there for the visit himself if it did take place the next day. At the end of the letter he sat down and wrote on the night, he tells Alexandrine that Desmoulin will be picking him up tomorrow morning ('at a quarter past eight') to have lunch with the Labori family in the country (Fernand Labori had been Zola's lawyer at his trial in 1898).

This Desmoulin duly did. The following letter, the very next evening, contains a long account of this pleasant day trip, how much he likes the family, how Labori persuaded them to stay for an extra-long walk, insisting that there was a train later than the one they had planned to get, which would still get them back to Paris in time for dinner; how Labori was wrong about the train—so that they were late back after all; but how really it didn't matter so much because it had been such a delightful day. So, not a disaster! In narrative terms, the minor muddle over the train timetable occupies an equivalent place to the smoke in the room on the previous evening.[64]

These different stories of daily disruptions at home and away are in tune with the dominant tone of Zola's letters to Alexandrine during this period. The underlying theme is that of a return to normality, following the year in England and the turbulence and frequent crises of the Dreyfus affair since the end of 1897. But Paris normality is very far from the ultra-quiet life of the London months, and Zola finds himself almost missing that isolation as he complains about the quantity of morning visits from people who want something from him, as well as the constant flow of invitations to social events. In retrospect, the period of exile now appears like a sort of idyllic research leave, the one time in his life when he was undistracted and able to get on with his work.

Another ongoing preoccupation during this time is the launch of *Fécondité*. It had already been published in instalments over the summer, in France and in some other countries too, with that pre-launch carefully timed to coincide with the return from exile and heralded by all those posters across the city, with their provocative picture of a luscious lactating *maman*. *Fécondité* finally came out as a book in October 1899. And Zola was itching to get down to working in earnest on his next novel, *Travail* (*Work*). So that now, with the Dreyfus process still taking time and attention, and given the contrast with the previous year in London, the peaceable passage of daily time becomes an explicit object: the dream of tranquillity as the daily *modus vivendi*, free from the importunity of others' demands or invitations. 'Just say no', his wife has been urging him, it seems, since Zola responds: 'You tell me it's quite simple to refuse. Is it possible to say no to everything, and will I really be able to shut my door?' 'No', he goes on, in answer to his own rhetorical questions. And suddenly with that door still ajar, we are transported to another world entirely, far away from the bustle and bother of working from home in the city:

> Non, l'incognito le plus absolu, comme pendant mon exil en Angleterre, serait le seul paradis.
>
> No, the most complete incognito, like during my exile in England, would be the only paradise.[65]

The *only* paradise: there is something compensatory, or disappointed, even in the perfection of heaven. 'No'. This paradise is not so much the one and only—as in, 'the girl of my dreams'—as the last place left in a world that withholds its sanctuary. But at the same time, and this is the real perversity of what is being said, exile in England has become an image not of the utmost deprivation, the most trying period of Zola's life—but, at the opposite end of the dreaming spectrum, the very model of Paradise: now forever lost.

Two years later, in 1901, the nostalgic re-vision of the London days is stated once more (Alexandrine is off again on her Italian roamings, hence a resumption of letter-writing):

> J'en arrive parfois à regretter la grande solitude où je me trouvais en Angleterre. Jamais de ma vie, je n'ai si bien travaillé, dans un plus grand calme.[66]
>
> There are moments when I find myself missing the great solitude of my time in England. Never in all my life have I worked so well, in a situation of greater calm.

The word 'great' in my translation fails to capture the lyrical tone of this *grande solitude* and then the *grand calme*, like the soothing tones of a lullaby. All the troubles and uncertainties of then are far away now. What remains is a sense of infinite expanse, of poetic solemnity; as if now this memory or this idyll were moving beyond the regretful hint of scarcity in the 'only paradise'. What we have here, looking backwards, is the lament for what has been lost, with the negative term to the fore, in all its hyperbolic superlativity. Never in all my life!

But in eleven more months—we are now at the start of November 1901—the latest and last long novel will have been written, and that earthly life, put out by another accident in the chimney, will be at an end. Ashes to ashes.

# NOTES

### Preface

1. Lionel Trilling, 'In Defense of Zola' (1953), in Trilling, *A Gathering of Fugitives* (London: Secker & Warburg, 1957), 12.
2. Angus Wilson, *Emile Zola: An Introductory Study of His Novels* (1952; London: Secker & Warburg, 1964), 33-4.
3. Wilson, *Emile Zola*, 34.
4. Wilson, *Emile Zola*, 35.
5. Wilson, *Emile Zola*, 35.
6. See F.W.J. Hemmings, *Émile Zola* (1953; 2nd edn. Oxford: Oxford University Press, 1966).
7. Naomi Schor, 'Introduction', *Yale French Studies* 42 (1969), 5; Hemmings, *Émile Zola*, n.p.
8. Michael Wood, 'Report from the Interior', *London Review of Books* 36:1 (9 January 2014). The book under review is Fredric Jameson, *The Antinomies of Realism* (London: Verso, 2013).

### Chapter 1

1. Émile Zola, *Au Bonheur des Dames* (1883), ed. Colette Becker (Paris: Garnier Flammarion, 1973), 112; *The Ladies' Paradise*, trans. Brian Nelson (Oxford: Oxford World's Classics, 1995), 78, tr. mod.
2. Rowan Williams, 'Icons and the Practice of Prayer', in *Holy Living: The Christian Tradition for Today* (London: Bloomsbury, 2017), 114-15.
3. Zola, 'Lettre à la jeunesse' ('Letter to Young People') (1879), in *Le Roman expérimental* (1880), ed., Aimé Guedj (Paris: Garnier Flammarion, 1971), 111.
4. See E.M. Forster, *Aspects of the Novel* (1927; London: Penguin, 1990), 73-81.

# NOTES

5. Zola, *La Joie de vivre* (1884), in Henri Mitterand (ed.), *Les Rougon Macquart*, vol. 3 (Paris: Pléiade, 1981), 1130; *The Bright Side of Life*, trans. Andrew Rothwell (Oxford: Oxford World's Classics, 2018), 305.
6. Zola, *Au Bonheur*, 113; *Paradise*, 79, tr. mod.
7. Andrew J. Counter, 'Zola's Repetitions: On Repetition in Zola', *Modern Language Review* 116: 1 (January 2021), 64.
8. Zola, *Au Bonheur*, 110; *Paradise*, 76, tr. mod.
9. Zola, *Paris* (1898), ed. Jacques Noiray (Paris: Folio, 2002), 579.
10. Zola, 'Causerie du dimanche', 3 December 1872 (from the newspaper *Le Corsaire*), in Adeline Wrona (ed.), *Zola journaliste: Articles et chroniques* (Paris: Éditions Flammarion, 2011), 206.
11. Zola, *Germinal*, in *Les Rougon Macquart*, vol. 3, 1133; *Germinal*, trans. Peter Collier (Oxford: Oxford World's Classics, 1993), 5.
12. Zola, *Germinal*, 1133; 5, tr. mod.
13. Zola, *Germinal*, 1134; 6.
14. Zola, *Germinal*, 1436; 348.
15. Zola, *Germinal*, 1434; 346.
16. Zola, *Thérèse Raquin* (1867), ed. Henri Mitterand (Paris: Garnier Flammarion, 1970), 67; trans. Andrew Rothwell (Oxford: Oxford World's Classics, 1992), 9.
17. Zola, *Thérèse Raquin*, 67; 9, tr. mod.
18. Zola, 'Préface de la deuxième édition' ('Preface to the Second Edition') (1868), *Thérèse Raquin*, 60; 2, tr. mod.
19. Zola, 'Le Roman expérimental' (1879), in *Le Roman expérimental*, 66.
20. Zola's research notes for each novel as well as the plans for their writing, including drawings, are accessible in published form: see Zola, *Carnets d'enquête: Une ethnographie inédite de la France*, ed. Henri Mitterand (Paris: France Loisirs, 1987); *Les Manuscrits et les dessins de Zola: Notes préparatoires et dessins des Rougon-Macquart*, eds. Olivier Lumbroso and Henri Mitterand, 3 vols. (Paris: Textuel, 2002).
21. William D. Wells, 'Computer Simulation of Consumer Behavior', in Edward C. Bursk and John F. Chapman (eds.), *Modern Marketing Strategy* (1964; New York: New American Library, 1965), 107–8.
22. Zola, *La Confession de Claude* (1865), ed. François-Marie Mourad (Paris: Livre de Poche, 2013), 188.
23. Zola, *Confession*, 190.

24. Zola, *Confession*, 190.
25. Zola, *Confession*, 190-1.
26. Zola, *Confession*, 193.
27. Zola, *Confession*, 217.
28. Zola, *Confession*, 217.
29. Zola, *Confession*, 219.
30. On the fantasy of the 'primal scene' of parental intercourse, see Freud's 'Wolf Man' case, *From the History of an Infantile Neurosis* (1918), in *Standard Edition*, trans. James Strachey, vol. 17 (1955; London: Hogarth Press, 1981), 48–60.
31. It is fitting, given Zola's visual awareness, that the required daily 'line' in this phrase may have been figurative rather than scriptural. It was cited by Pliny the Elder as being derived from the Greek painter Apelles. On this intricate genealogy, see Susan Harrow, 'Worlds of Work and the Work of Words: Zola', in Marcus Waithe and Claire White (eds.), *The Labour of Literature in Britain and France, 1830–1910: Authorial Work Ethics* (London: Palgrave Macmillan, 2018), 207.
32. On Zola's representation of the power of the press within his novels, see Kate Rees, 'Zola: Ambiguities, Battles, Jolts', in *The Journalist in the French Fin-de-siècle: Enfants de la Presse* (Oxford: MHRA/Legenda, 2018), 52–94. As Rees says (p. 53), 'More than any other writer of the period ... Zola's career is intimately bound up with journalism and its developments in the later decades of the nineteenth century.'
33. See Zola, 'L'Argent dans la littérature', in Aimé Guedj (ed.), *Le Roman expérimental* (1880) (Paris: Garnier Flammarion, 1971), 175–210.
34. Zola, '*Le Supplice d'une femme* et *Les Deux Sœurs*', in François-Marie Mourad (ed.), *Mes Haines* (1866) (Paris: Garnier Flammarion, 2012), 196.
35. Zola, 'Supplice', 197.
36. Zola, 'Supplice', 196.
37. Zola, '*Germinie Lacerteux*, par MM. Ed. et J. de Goncourt', in *Mes haines*, 95.
38. Zola, *Confession*, 231.
39. Just about: in recent years, critics have begun to explore the blind spots and swift elisions in Zola's rare mentions (they are not more than that) of non-white or non-French characters. See, for instance, Jean-Marie Seillan, 'L'Afrique utopique de *Fécondité*', *Cahiers naturalistes*

75 (2001), 183–202; and Jennifer Yee, 'Émile Zola's Black Lives: Colonial Experiments and the Limits of Empathy in *La Joie de vivre*', *Dix-Neuf* 28:1 (2022), 1–15.

40. Incestuous connections remain a preoccupation in many of the Rougon-Macquart novels as well, not least *Le Docteur Pascal* (1893), the last of the cycle, in which the scientist uncle—the doctor—has a baby with the niece, Clothilde, who has come to live with him. See also Nicholas White, 'Incest in "Les Rougon-Macquart"', in *The Family in Crisis in Late Nineteenth-Century French Fiction* (Cambridge: Cambridge University Press, 1999), 98–123.
41. Zola, *Madeleine Férat* (1868; Paris: Livre de Poche, 1972), 305.
42. Zola, *Madeleine Férat*, 35.
43. Zola, *Madeleine Férat*, 136.
44. Zola, *Madeleine Férat*, 303.
45. Zola, *Madeleine Férat*, 308.
46. With an equally ironic title to *Une page d'amour*, the bleakly moving *Une belle journée* (*A Beautiful Day*) (1881), by Zola's friend Henry Céard, plays in a similar way with characters' own expectations of an adultery story. Céard's Mme Duhamain is a sort of Madame Bovary *manquée*. Bored with her unromantic husband, she spends hours not in fact having sex with her would-be lover, Trudon; they wait out a rainy day in a restaurant's upstairs private dining room which, as with the rented rooms in *Une page d'amour*, is set up for the casual seduction which in this case does not come about.
47. Zola, *Une page d'amour* (1878), ed. Pierre Marotte (Paris: Livre de Poche, 1985), 276; *A Love Story*, trans. Helen Constantine (Oxford: Oxford World's Classics, 2017), 205, tr. mod.

## Chapter 2

1. Brian Nicholas, 'The Novel as Social Document: *L'Assommoir* (1877)', in Ian Gregor and Nicholas, *The Moral and the Story* (London: Faber and Faber, 1962), 66. It is fair to guess that had this been written today rather than in the 1960s, that generic 'him' would have been 'them' or 'him or her': the writing milieu is an evolving context, too.

2. First broadcast on BBC One in 1992, *Absolutely Fabulous* starred Jennifer Saunders and Joanna Lumley as ageing celebrities of the fashion industry.
3. See Michael B. Miller, *The Bon Marché: Bourgeois Culture and the Department Store, 1869–1920* (London: George Allen & Unwin, 1981).
4. *Il Paradiso delle signore* follows the fortunes of a shop in Milan; it began in 2015 and has had eight seasons to date. *The Paradise*, set in the north-east of England, was broadcast on BBC One in 2012 (and on PBS in the US in 2013). Also in English, there was a year-long dramatization, beginning in late 2015, of the entire Rougon-Macquart series on BBC Radio 4 entitled *Blood, Sex and Money*; as that title suggests, this was not a version that concentrated on Zola as a writer about ordinary life.
5. On *Nana*'s attractions, see Peter Brooks, 'Nana at Last Unveil'd? Problems of the Modern Nude', in *Body Work* (Cambridge, MA: Harvard University Press, 1993), 123–61.
6. Zola, *Thérèse Raquin* (1867), ed. Henri Mitterand (Paris: Garnier Flammarion, 1970), 66; trans. Andrew Rothwell (Oxford: Oxford World's Classics, 1992), 8. On the profile of Thérèse, see Chapter 1, 22-4.
7. Zola, *Thérèse Raquin*, 65; 7.
8. Despite the coalescence of their interests in topics such as the crowd, the city, and the commodity in nineteenth-century Paris, Benjamin makes just a single reference to Zola in the extensive notes and manuscripts for the uncompleted work known as the Arcades Project. In the section explicitly on Paris *passages* there is a brief paragraph on how the arcades were already dying at the time of *Thérèse Raquin*: see Walter Benjamin, *Das Passagen-Werk*, ed. Rolf Tiedemann (Frankfurt am Main: Suhrkamp, 1982), vol. 2, 1046; *The Arcades Project*, trans. Howard Eiland and Kevin McLaughlin (Cambridge, MA: Harvard University Press, 2002). In the 1935 plan for 'Paris, Capital of the Nineteenth Century' there is one elliptical sentence in which Zola is said to take up Fourier's phalanstery model of social organization in his last novel, *Travail* (*Work*) (1901), just as he is taking leave of the arcades in *Thérèse Raquin*: see *Das Passagen-Werk*, vol. 1, 47. But there is not a word on *Au Bonheur des Dames*, Zola's dissection of modern shopping developments—despite that aspect of recent history being central

to Benjamin's twentieth-century investigation. On this absence, see further Nicholas Rennie, 'Benajmin and Zola: Narrative, the Individual, and Crowds in an Age of Mass Production', *Comparative Literature Studies* 33: 4 (1996), 396–413; Adrian Rifkin, 'Total Ellipsis: Zola, Benjamin and the Dialectics of Kitsch', *Parallax* 2: 1 (1996), 101–13.
9. Zola, *Thérèse Raquin*, 66; 7–8.
10. Zola, *Thérèse Raquin*, 66; 8.
11. Zola, *Thérèse Raquin*, 132; 76, tr. mod.
12. Zola, *Thérèse Raquin*, 131–2; 76.
13. On that second twentieth-century retailing revolution, see Rachel Bowlby, *Carried Away: The Invention of Modern Shopping* (London: Faber and Faber, 2000); and for subsequent developments, Bowlby, *Back to the Shops: The High Street in History and the Future* (Oxford: Oxford University Press, 2022).
14. Zola, *Au Bonheur des Dames* (1883; Paris: Garnier Flammarion, 1971), 43; *The Ladies' Paradise*, trans. Brian Nelson (Oxford: Oxford World's Classics, 1995), 5, tr. mod.
15. Zola, *Au Bonheur*, 87; *Paradise*, 51, tr. mod.
16. Zola, *Au Bonheur*, 209; *Paradise*, 181.
17. Zola, *Au Bonheur*, 133; *Paradise*, 101, tr. mod.
18. Zola, *Au Bonheur*, 133; *Paradise*, 101, tr. mod.
19. Zola, *Au Bonheur*, 133; *Paradise*, 101.
20. Zola, *Au Bonheur*, 200–1; *Paradise*, 173, tr. mod.
21. See Zola, *La Joie de vivre* (1884), in *Œuvres complètes*, ed. Henri Mitterand, vol. 3 (Paris: Pléiade, 1964), 1023; *The Bright Side of Life*, trans. Andrew Rothwell (Oxford: Oxford World's Classics, 2018), 205.
22. Susan Harrow describes Gervaise's loving care for and admiration of this clock in its every detail once she really possesses it: how she 'lavish[es] attention on its case, its texture, its mechanism, and its name'; *Zola, the Body Modern: Pressures and Prospects of Representation* (2010; London: Routledge, 2020), 178. There may also be a gentle authorial identification in the background. In *Zola's Painters* (Oxford: MHRA/Legenda, 2022), Robert Lethbridge describes Cézanne's painting, in 1870, of a clock of Zola's as indicative of the author's 'increasingly bourgeois comforts' at this time (p. 48). Much later, in letters to Alexandrine, he discusses how the best souvenirs to bring back from holidays

# NOTES

are objects for everyday use that will be handled and cherished all the time. For example, there is this charming paragraph—Zola window-shopping in Upper Norwood!—from the last weeks of the period in England:

> Yesterday, Saturday, I gave myself a little present. I bought myself, as a container for my *langues de chat*, a biscuit tin that I had been seeing for a while in the window of the shop where we bought that spoon for you, that you left here for me. I liked it a lot, and it is very pretty. As it will have been something I used during my exile, it will be a souvenir for me.

(Zola, *Lettres à Alexandrine 1876–1901*, ed. Brigitte Émile-Zola and Alain Pagès (Paris: Gallimard, 2014), 465, letter of Sunday 23 April 1899.)

23. Zola, *L'Assommoir* (1877), ed. Jacques Dubois (Paris: Garnier Flammarion, 1969), 156; *The Assommoir*, trans. Brian Nelson (Oxford: Oxford World's Classics, 2021), 121, tr. mod.
24. Zola, *L'Assommoir*, 156; 121, tr. mod.
25. Zola, *L'Assommoir*, 157; 121.
26. Zola, *L'Assommoir*, 180; 143, tr. mod.
27. Zola, *L'Assommoir*, 180; 143–4, tr. mod.
28. Zola, *L'Assommoir*, 326; 282, tr. mod.
29. Zola, *L'Assommoir*, 380–1; 333, tr. mod.
30. Zola, *L'Assommoir*, 381; 334, tr. mod.
31. Zola, *L'Assommoir*, 397; 349, tr. mod.
32. Zola, *L'Assommoir*, 438; 389, tr. mod.
33. Zola, *Le Ventre de Paris* (1873), ed. Henri Mitterand (Paris: Folio, 1990), 98; trans. Brian Nelson, *The Belly of Paris* (Oxford: Oxford World's Classics, 2007), 50, tr. mod. On the depiction of the new Les Halles market in this novel, see Geoff Woollen, 'Zola's Halles, a *Grande Surface* before Their Time', *Romance Studies* 18: 1 (June 2000), 21–30.
34. Zola, *Le Ventre*, 97; *Belly*, 49, tr. mod.
35. The number of Gervaise's children is a rare instance of Zola changing his mind and his plan in the preparations for the Rougon-Macquart cycle (the writing of which was itself an undertaking across two decades). To begin with, in *L'Assommoir*, the novel of Gervaise herself, there are three of them. Later, a fourth child (and third son) is added,

## NOTES

Jacques Lantier, who is the protagonist of *La Bête humaine*. See further Daniel Ferrer, 'Combien d'enfants avait Lady Gervaise? Le style de l'invention dans les ébauches de Zola', in Jean-Pierre Leduc-Adine (ed.), *Zola: Genèse de l'œuvre* (Paris: CNRS Éditions, 2002), 17-32.

36. Zola, *Le Ventre*, 100; *Belly*, 51, tr. mod.
37. Zola, *Le Ventre*, 118-19; *Belly*, 64, tr. mod.

## Chapter 3

1. Émile Zola, *Lettres à Alexandrine, 1876-1901*, eds. Brigitte Émile-Zola and Alain Pagès (Paris: Gallimard, 2014), 606-7, 618, letters of Friday 10 and Tuesday 14 November 1899.
2. See Robert Harris, *An Officer and a Spy* (London: Hutchinson, 2013). The novel is focussed on the life of one of the key witnesses in the campaign to clear Dreyfus, Colonel Georges Picquart. The title, referring both to Picquart and to the accusation of espionage wrongly levelled at Dreyfus, plays on that of the 1982 movie *An Officer and a Gentleman*. In French, the Polanski film is called instead *J'Accuse*. Zola himself makes only a cameo appearance as a character in it, but the name of his article of 1898 can still immediately evoke the force of the Dreyfusard campaign.
3. There is an extensive historical literature on the Dreyfus affair, which continues to evolve. Two notable recent works in English are Ruth Harris, *The Man on Devil's Island: Alfred Dreyfus and the Affair that Divided France* (New Haven, CT: Yale University Press, 2011) and (on Dreyfus himself) Maurice Samuels, *Alfred Dreyfus: The Man at the Center of the Affair* (New Haven, CT: Yale University Press, 2024). On Zola's English exile, see Michael Rosen, *The Disappearance of Emile Zola: Love, Literature and the Dreyfus Case* (London: Faber, 2017).
4. See Ernest Alfred Vizetelly, *With Zola in England: A Story of Exile* (London: Chatto & Windus, 1999), 18.
5. Zola, *Pages d'exil*, ed. Colin Burns, in Zola, *Œuvres complètes*, ed. Henri Mitterand, vol. 14 (Paris: Cercle du Livre Précieux, 1970), 1153-4. Burns's edition of the *Pages d'exil* was published only in the 1960s, in the academic periodical *Nottingham French Studies* 3: 1 (May 1964), 2-46. Zola had intended to amplify the notes of his journal and make a book of it, but had not yet done this at the time of his death in 1902. Sixty years

later (and sixty years ago today), its English publication (in French) was the first.

In the 1890s women who bicycle are an image of progressive social movement for Zola. In a delightful scene towards the end of *Paris*, Pierre Froment's ongoing delivery from the fetters of his priestly vocation is demonstrated by way of an exhilarating Sunday initiation into the joys of cycling, under the instruction of the charming Marie—who, by the end of the novel, will be his wife and the mother of their baby: see *Paris* (1898), ed. Jacques Noiray (Paris: Folio, 2002), 451.

6. See Vizetelly, *With Zola in England*, 29–30: 'By this time, however, we had reached St. James's Park, and there, as we seated ourselves on some chairs beside the ornamental water, I led the conversation into another channel by producing an evening newspaper, and reading therefrom successive narratives of how M. Zola had sailed for Norway, how he had taken train at the Eastern Terminus in Paris, and how he had been bicycling through the Oberland on his way to some mysterious Helvetian retreat. Then we laughed—ah! those journalists!—and fears were at an end.'

7. There is the (literally) horrible judgement of Henry James, recalling his impression of Zola in the early 1890s as 'fairly bristling with the betrayal that nothing whatever had happened to him in life but to write *Les Rougon-Macquart*'; 'Emile Zola', in Morris Shapira (ed.), *Selected Literary Criticism* (1963; Cambridge: Cambridge University Press, 1981), 243.

8. Zola, 'L'Encre et le sang' ('Ink and Blood') (1880), in Adeline Wrona (ed.), *Zola journaliste: Articles et chroniques* (Paris: Éditions Flammarion, 2011), 298.

9. See Evelyne Bloch-Dano, *Madame Zola* (1997; Paris: Grasset, 1998); also Graham Robb, 'Madame Zola', in *Parisians: An Adventure History of Paris* (London: Picador, 2010), 175–97.

10. Letters to Jeanne from the first years of her relationship with Zola do not survive; they were taken by Alexandrine when she first learned of the relationship shortly after the birth of Jacques, in late 1891.

11. See Brigitte Émile-Zola, 'Avant-Propos', in Zola, *Lettres à Alexandrine*, 8–9.

12. Zola, *Lettres à Alexandrine*, 486, Thursday 11 May 1899.

13. Zola, *Lettres à Alexandrine*, 488, Thursday 11 May 1899.

14. Zola, *Lettres à Jeanne Rozerot*, 252–3, Thursday 22 December 1898.
15. Zola, *Lettres à Jeanne Rozerot*, 247, Thursday 15 December 1898.
16. Zola, *Lettres à Jeanne Rozerot*, 214, Sunday 23 October 1898.
17. Zola, *Lettres à Alexandrine*, 483, Tuesday 9 May 1899.
18. On Zola's daily writing habits, see Alain Pagès, 'Comment Zola écrivait-il?', in Jean-Pierre Leduc-Adine (ed.), *Zola: Genèse de l'œuvre* (Paris: CNRS Éditions, 2002), 281–91.
19. Zola, *Lettres à Jeanne Rozerot*, 214, Sunday 23 October 1898.
20. Zola, *Lettres à Jeanne Rozerot*, 288–9, Thursday 9 February 1899.
21. Zola, *Lettres à Jeanne Rozerot*, 289, Thursday 9 February, 1899.
22. See Virginia Woolf, 'Professions for Women' (1931), in Rachel Bowlby (ed.), *The Crowded Dance of Modern Life* (London: Penguin, 1993), 101.
23. The regularity of the work, line after line and hour after hour, makes it in this respect more like a factory job than a profession, with varying occupations and activities. Claire White makes the connection via the late novel *Travail* (*Work*) in which 'the familiar and unfailing metre of material work provides an appropriate metaphor for Zola's own linguistic idealism': the mastery of language is the mastery of a work process; White, *Work and Leisure in Late Nineteenth-Century French Culture* (London: Palgrave Macmillan, 2014), 198.
24. Zola, *Lettres à Jeanne Rozerot*, 214–15, Sunday 23 October 1898.
25. Many of the photographs taken by Zola in England are reproduced in *Emile Zola: Photographer in Norwood, South London, 1898–1899* (Croydon: Norwood Society, 1997), obtainable from The Norwood Society, www.norwoodsociety.co.uk. See also François Émile-Zola and Massin, *Zola photographe* (Paris: Denoël, 1979) and Mathilde Falguière-Léonard et al. (eds.), *Zola et la photographie* (Paris: Herrmann, 2023). For a precise account of the relationships between photography and literary realism, see Jill Kelly, 'Photographic Reality and French Literary Realism: Nineteenth-Century Synchronism and Symbiosis', *French Review* 65: 2 (December 1991), 195–205.
26. In a letter to Alexandrine on Sunday 7 August 1898, Zola says that he has already done twenty pages of his novel, begun three days before; Zola, *Lettres à Alexandrine*, 305.
27. In July 1880 Edmond Goncourt writes in his *Journal*: 'Coming back from Médan I say to myself that a home can do without children in a Paris apartment, but not in a country house'; quoted in Bloch-Dano, 158n2.

28. Andrew J. Counter notes the paradoxically 'tetragenic' proclivities of Zola's celebration of life, 'which generate such a rich profusion of monstrous scapegoats and cautionary tales. The intolerance displayed by Zola's reproductive politics in dealing with these phantasmatic creations is, at times, disturbing'; 'Zola's *Fin-de-Siècle* Reproductive Politics', *French Studies* 68: 2 (April 2014), 208.
29. Zola, *Fécondité* (Paris: Charpentier, 1899), 78. Larry Duffy usefully describes the complex classificatory grid of Zola's terminology in relation to *froideur* and related categories: 'Some [women] are reproductively impotent, some are orgasmically impotent; some are cold in terms of desire, others in terms of pleasure; some are intentionally sterile, others unintentionally. Like *froideur*, impotence can apply to desire or pleasure, but it can also denote sterility, as can be seen in a range of women with various sexual and/or reproductive issues—almost always the consequence of nature-thwarting frauds or surgery'; Duffy, 'Medical Humanism or *Scientia Sexualis*? Building a Sexological Concept in *Fécondité*', *Nottingham French Studies* 60: 3 (2021), 327.
30. See Freud, *Three Essays on the Theory of Sexuality* (1905), trans. James Strachey, in *Standard Edition of the Complete Works of Sigmund Freud*, vol. 7 (London: Hogarth Press, 1953), esp. 149–72.
31. Zola, 'Dépopulation' (1896), in *Œuvres complètes*, vol. 14, 788.
32. See Alain Drouard, 'Aux origines de l'eugénisme en France: le néo-malthusianisme (1896–1914)', *Population* 47: 2 (March–April 1992), 435–59.
33. Zola, *Fécondité*, 498.
34. Zola, *Lettres à Alexandrine*, 484, Tuesday 9 May 1899.
35. See Zola, *Fécondité*, 493.
36. Zola, *Fécondité*, 508.
37. Zola, *Fécondité*, 509.
38. Zola, *Fécondité*, 505; ellipses in original.
39. Zola, *Fécondité*, 282.
40. Zola, *Fécondité*, 256.
41. Zola, *Fécondité*, 293.
42. Wet-nursing is now a practice of the past in the Western countries where it was standard in Zola's time. But other, related arguments about pre- and post-natal motherhood often still echo those outlined

in *Fécondité*—from 'breast is best' (as opposed to formula milk) to the protest against a class-based refusal of physical maternity: 'too posh to push' (against planned Caesarean deliveries). And to the extent that wet-nursing physically replaces one mother's body with that of another, so surrogacy does the same thing, for the months of pregnancy. Like wet-nursing in its time, surrogacy—in jurisdictions where it is legal—is typically organized through profit-making agencies which may exploit both the intending parents and the women who do the job. In the UK surrogacy is legal on an 'expenses only' basis; it must not be paid work. In France it is not legal. I wrote about contemporary issues surrounding surrogacy and reproductive technologies in *A Child of One's Own: Parental Stories* (Oxford: Oxford University Press, 2013), 35–64.

43. Charles Péguy, quoted in David Baguley, '*Fécondité' d'Emile Zola: Roman à thèse, évangile, mythe* (Toronto: University of Toronto Press, 1973), 158, 159.
44. On the contradictions and confusions of the African finale, see Jean-Marie Seillan, 'L'Afrique utopique de *Fécondité*', *Cahiers naturalistes* 75 (2001), 183–202.
45. See Zola, *Fécondité*, 738–9.
46. Zola, *Fécondité*, 751. At just one point in the speech of the grandson visiting from Africa, Dominique, there is a hint of possible conflict in the adopted or colonized region. This is owing to 'religious fanaticism, aggravating the great difficulty of our conquest, this terrible problem of Islam, which we will come up against for as long as it is not resolved'; Zola, *Fecondité*, 741.
47. Zola, *Lettres à Alexandrine*, 486, Thursday 11 May 1899.
48. On the poster publicity, see Zola, *Lettres à Alexandrine*, 462, Saturday 22 April 1899. Other state-of-the-art promotion for *Fécondité* included a forty-day contract for night-time electric-light beaming of the words 'Lisez Fécondité, par Émile Zola' ('Read *Fécondité*, by Émile Zola') at a prime intersection of boulevards in the centre of Paris; see Henri Mitterand, *Zola*, vol. III, *L'Honneur, 1893–1902* (Paris: Fayard, 2002), 662. The twenty Rougon-Macquarts, and recently some of the late, long novels too, are available in affordable French paperback editions. But of all Zola's novels, *Fécondité* shares with *Travail* the sad distinction

of not having ever been issued in that form, although a scholarly edition of *Fécondité*, edited by Marie Lapière and running to just short of 1,000 pages, was published in 2023 by Classiques Garnier. There was also, in 1979, an edition of just the first section of *Travail*, published by Verdier, with a collective preface—flagged up on the cover—written by workers at the Lip watch factory cooperative in Besançon. The novels of the *Trois Villes* (*Three Cities*) trilogy, *Paris*, *Lourdes*, and *Rome*, have all been edited by Jacques Noiray as Folio Classique paperbacks; likewise, *Vérité* (*Truth*) (1903), the posthumously published Paris novel about antisemitism, loosely derived from the Dreyfus affair, was reissued in 1995 in the Livre de Poche collection. In English, the only translation of *Fécondité* ever to appear was Ernest Vizetelly's, called *Fruitfulness*, in 1900, not long after the novel's first publication in French. This is a much truncated and 'adapted' version, in part to avoid the risk of the prosecution for obscene libel incurred in 1888 by his father, Henry Vizetelly, for his publication of *The Soil*, a translation of Zola's *La Terre*, and then in 1889 for several other novels, including two by Zola: see Peter Keating, *The Haunted Study: A Social History of the English Novel 1875–1914* (1989; London: Fontana, 1991), 244–5.

49. Zola, *Lettres à Alexandrine*, 487, Thursday 11 May 1899.
50. Zola, *Lettres à Alexandrine*, 488, Thursday 11 May 1899. The triple dog-wolf-cat, *chien-loup-chat*, is the pet name that Émile and Alexandrine use reciprocally for each other. In his preface to the *Lettres à Alexandrine* (pp. 27–8), Alain Pagès beautifully describes the significance of this mutual endearment. The couple had cats and dogs throughout their life together; Zola's novels are full of animals who are characters in their own right, and had recently written a newspaper column on 'The Love of Animals', suggesting that this shared human feeling might serve as a beginning for the breakdown of international conflict: 'From this universal love of animals, beyond frontiers, perhaps we could get to the universal love of people'; 'L'Amour des bêtes', *Œuvres complètes*, vol. 14, 741. The death of their dog Pin in September 1898, while Zola was away, is movingly evoked in the sequence of letters that describe his response to the news (and before that, the fear of it). In the spring of 1999 Alexandrine took in a stray cat and the two of them discussed

in their letters what to call it; the name chosen is that of a character from *Fécondité*, Moineaud.
51. Zola, *Lettres à Alexandrine*, 530, Thursday 12 October 1899.
52. 'Desmoulin prétend que des anti-dreyfusards sont montés sur le toit boucher nos cheminées'; Zola, *Lettres à Alexandrine*, 530, Thursday 12 October 1899.
53. See Franz Kafka, *The Metamorphosis* (1915), in Kafka, *The Metamorphosis and Other Stories*, trans. Joyce Crick (Oxford: Oxford World's Classics, 2009), 29–74.
54. Zola, *La Conquête de Plassans* (1874), ed. Pierre Marotte (Paris: Livre de Poche, 1984), 421; *The Conquest of Plassans*, trans. Helen Constantine (Oxford: Oxford World's Classics, 2014), 288, tr. mod.
55. Zola, *Conquête*, 435; *Conquest*, 298, tr. mod.
56. Zola, *Conquête*, 436; *Conquest*, 299, tr. mod.
57. Zola, *Conquête*, 206; *Conquest*, 140, tr. mod.
58. Zola, *Conquête*, 207; *Conquest*, 141.
59. Sigmund Freud, *The Complete Letters of Sigmund Freud to Wilhelm Fliess, 1887–1904*, trans. Jeffrey Moussaieff Masson (Cambridge, MA: Harvard University Press, 1985), 410, letter of 25 April 1900.
60. Freud, ' Contribution to a Questionnaire on Reading' (1907), trans. James Strachey, *Standard Edition*, vol. 9 (1959; London: Hogarth Press, 1981), 246.
61. Freud, ' Observations on Transference-Love (Further Recommendations on the Technique of Psycho-Analysis)' (1915), *Standard Edition*, trans. James Strachey, vol. 12 (1958; London: Hogarth Press, 1991), 162; 'Bemerkungen über die Übertragungsliebe', *Gesammelte Werke*, vol. 10 (Frankfurt: Fischer, 1999), 309–10.
62. Freud, 'Observations', 168; 'Bemerkungen', 317.
63. Freud, *The Interpretation of Dreams* (1900), *Standard Edition*, vol. 5 (1953; London: Hogarth Press, 1991), 509.
64. Zola does say, in the letter written the following evening, that on his return from the long day out Jules, the servant, reported that the heating was working fine now in both rooms, and that the smoke in the study had been due to some plaster falling and blocking it; see *Lettres à Alexandrine*, 532.
65. Zola, *Lettres à Alexandrine*, 638, Wednesday 22 November 1899.
66. Zola, *Lettres à Alexandrine*, 729, Monday 4 November 1901.

# ACKNOWLEDGEMENTS

Most of all, I would like to thank Anne Cheng for her perfectly timed invitation, as one of its editors, to contribute to the *My Reading* series—just when I had begun a new phase of reading and thinking about Zola. Going back to much earlier inspiration, it is a pleasure to thank Fredric Jameson who long ago told me I had to read Zola's *Au Bonheur des Dames*; and then, one result of that, to thank again Chantal Laquintat and M. Simonnot, who welcomed me into their attic architectural office at the Bon Marché department store to pore over its nineteenth-century archives—the same documents that Zola would have been looking at in the research for writing his novel.

Both recently and in the longer term, I am immensely grateful to students for all their responses to reading Zola—and for demonstrating in ever different ways the multi-faceted appeal of *Au Bonheur des Dames*, in particular. Conversations with friends and colleagues, and invitations to give talks, have helped me to shape the book—and just to get on with writing it. Here once again I thank Anne Cheng; also Peter Brooks, Mairéad Hanrahan, Margaret Homans, Susan Harrow, Chantal Morel, Deborah Nord, Susan Sellers, and Rebecca Sugden. Melvyn Harrison of the Crystal Palace Foundation kindly shared some of his knowledge of the local history surrounding Zola's eleven months living in Upper Norwood, in 1898-9.

Warm thanks as well are due to Jack McNichol and Aimee Wright at Oxford University Press for their thoughtful support throughout the process of preparation, and to Sally Evans-Darby for her careful copy-editing. Also, I thank Rajeswari Azayecoche for her flexible and efficient management of the book's production.

# BIBLIOGRAPHY

*Editions of Zola's novels (in French and in English translation, where applicable) are not listed here, but are given in the endnotes to each chapter.*

Baguley, David, *'Fécondité' d'Émile Zola: Roman à thèse, évangile, mythe* (Toronto: University of Toronto Press, 1973)

Baudelaire, Charles, *Le Peintre de la vie moderne* (1863), in Marcel A. Ruff (ed.), *Œuvres complètes* (Paris: Éditions du Seuil, 1968), 546–65

Benjamin, Walter, *Das Passagen-Werk*, 2 vols., ed. Rolf Tiedemann (Frankfurt am Main: Suhrkamp, 1982)

Birch, Edmund, *Fictions of the Press in Nineteenth-Century France* (London: Palgrave Macmillan, 2018)

Bowlby, Rachel, *Back to the Shops: The High Street in History and the Future* (Oxford: Oxford University Press, 2022)

Bowlby, Rachel, *Carried Away: The Invention of Modern Shopping* (London: Faber and Faber, 2000)

Bowlby, Rachel, *A Child of One's Own: Parental Stories* (Oxford: Oxford University Press, 2013)

Bowlby, Rachel, *Just Looking: Consumer Culture in Dreiser, Gissing and Zola* (1985; rpt. London: Routledge, 2009)

Brooks, Peter, 'Nana at Last Unveil'd? Problems of the Modern Nude', in *Body Work* (Cambridge, MA: Harvard University Press, 1993), 123–6

Céard, Henry, *Une belle journée* (1881), ed. C.A. Burns (Geneva: Slatkine, 1980)

Counter, Andrew J., 'Zola's *Fin-de-Siècle* Reproductive Politics', *French Studies* 68: 2 (April 2014), 193–208

Counter, Andrew J., 'Zola's Repetitions: On Repetition in Zola', *Modern Language Review* 116: 1 (January 2021), 42–64

Darwin, Charles, *On the Origin of Species* (1859), ed. Gillian Beer (Oxford: Oxford World's Classics, 1998)

## BIBLIOGRAPHY

Drouard, Alain, 'Aux origines de l'eugénisme en France: le néomalthusianisme (1896–1914)', *Population* 47: 2 (March–April 1992), 435–59

Duffy, Larry, 'Medical Humanism or *Scientia Sexualis*? Building a Sexological Concept in *Fécondité*', *Nottingham French Studies* 60: 3 (2021), 317–33

Émile-Zola, François, and Massin, *Zola photographe* (Paris: Denoël, 1979)

Falguière-Léonard, Mathiled et al. (eds.), *Zola et la photographie* (Paris: Herrmann, 2023)

Ferrer, Daniel, 'Combien d'enfants avait Lady Gervaise? Le style de l'invention dans les ébauches de Zola', in Jean-Pierre Leduc-Adine (ed.), *Zola: Genèse de l'œuvre* (Paris: CNRS Éditions, 2002), 17–32

Foster, Kate, 'Lèche-vitrines: Human Identity and the Mannequin in Zola's *Au Bonheur des Dames*', *Dix-Neuf* 26: 2 (2022), 74–90

Freud, Sigmund, *The Complete Letters of Sigmund Freud to Wilhelm Fliess, 1887–1904*, trans. Jeffrey Moussaieff Masson (Cambridge, MA: Harvard University Press, 1985)

Freud, Sigmund, 'Contribution to a Questionnaire on Reading' (1907), in *Standard Edition of the Complete Psychological Works of Sigmund Freud*, trans. James Strachey, vol. 9 (1959; London: Hogarth Press, 1981), 245–7

Freud, Sigmund, *From the History of an Infantile Neurosis* (1918) ('The Wolf Man'), in *Standard Edition*, vol. 17 (1955; London: Hogarth Press, 1981), 7–122

Freud, Sigmund, *The Interpretation of Dreams* (1900), in *Standard Edition*, vol. 5 (1953; London: Hogarth Press, 1991)

Freud, Sigmund, 'Observations on Transference-Love (Further Recommendations on the Technique of Psycho-Analysis)' (1915), in *Standard Edition*, vol. 12 (1958; London: Hogarth Press, 1991), 159–71

Freud, Sigmund, *Three Essays on the Theory of Sexuality* (1905), in *Standard Edition*, vol. 7 (1953; London: Hogarth Press, 1991), 130–243

Harris, Robert, *An Officer and a Spy* (London: Hutchinson, 2013)

Harris, Ruth, *The Man on Devil's Island: Alfred Dreyfus and the Affair That Divided France* (New Haven, CT: Yale University Press, 2011)

Harrow, Susan, 'Living Alone Together: Barthes, Zola, and the Work of Letters', *L'Esprit Créateur* 55: 4 (Winter 2015), 21–38

Harrow, Susan, '*Thérèse Raquin*: Animal Passion and the Brutality of Reading', in Brian Nelson (ed.), *Cambridge Companion to Émile Zola* (Cambridge: Cambridge University Press, 2007), 105–20

## BIBLIOGRAPHY

Harrow, Susan, 'Worlds of Work and the Work of Words: Zola', in Marcus Waithe and Claire White (eds.), *The Labour of Literature in Britain and France, 1830–1910: Authorial Work Ethics* (London: Palgrave Macmillan, 2018), 203–19

Harrow, Susan, *Zola, the Body Modern: Pressures and Prospects of Representation* (2010; rpt. London: Routledge, 2020)

Hemmings, F.W.J., *Emile Zola* (1953; 2nd ed. Oxford: Oxford University Press, 1966)

James, Henry, 'Emile Zola' (1903), in Morris Shapira (ed.), *Selected Literary Criticism* (1963; Cambridge: Cambridge University Press, 1981), 240–64

Jefferson, Ann, 'Creativity and Procreation in Zola's *L'Œuvre*', in *Genius in France: An Idea and Its Uses* (Princeton, NJ: Princeton University Press, 2014), 146–57

Kafka, Franz, *The Metamorphosis* (1915), in Kafka, *The Metamorphosis and Other Stories*, trans. Joyce Crick (Oxford: Oxford World's Classics, 2009), 29–74

Keating, Peter, *The Haunted Study: A Social History of the English Novel 1875–1914* (1989; London: Fontana, 1991)

Kelly, Jill, 'Henry Céard: Photographs of an Affair', *Nineteenth-Century French Studies* 24: 1–2 (Fall–Winter 1995–6), 203–16

Kelly, Jill, 'Photographic Reality and French Literary Realism: Nineteenth-Century Synchronism and Symbiosis', *French Review* 65: 2 (December 1991), 195–205

Lethbridge, Robert, *Zola's Painters* (Oxford: MHRA/Legenda, 2022)

Marcus, Sharon, 'Zola's Restless House', in *Apartment Stories: City and Home in Nineteenth-Century Paris and London* (Berkeley, CA: University of California Press, 1999), 166–98

Mehlman, Jeffrey, 'The Dreyfus Affair', in Denis Hollier (ed.), *A New History of French Literature* (1989; rpt. Cambridge, MA: Harvard University Press, 1994), 824–30

Miller, Michael B., *The Bon Marché: Bourgeois Culture and the Department Store, 1869–1920* (London: George Allen & Unwin, 1981)

Mitterand, Henri, *Zola et le naturalisme* (1986; 4th ed. Paris: PUF, 2016)

Mitterand, Henri, *Zola*, vol. 3, *L'Honneur, 1893–1902* (Paris: Fayard, 2002)

Nicholas, Brian, 'The Novel as Social Document: *L'Assommoir* (1877)', in Ian Gregor and Nicholas (eds.), *The Moral and the Story* (London: Faber and Faber, 1962), 63–97

Nicholas, Brian, 'Zola', in John Cruikshank (ed.), *French Literature and Its Background, 5: The Late Nineteenth Century* (Oxford: Oxford University Press, 1969), 154–72

Pagès, Alain, 'Comment Zola écrivait-il?', in Jean-Pierre Leduc-Adine (ed.), *Zola: Genèse de l'œuvre* (Paris: CNRS Éditions, 2002), 281–91

Pagès, Alain, *Émile Zola: De 'J'accuse' au Panthéon* (Paris: Lucien Souny, 2008)

Pagès, Alain, *Zola et le groupe de Médan: Histoire d'un cercle littéraire* (Paris: Perrin, 2014)

Rees, Kate, 'Zola: Ambiguities, Battles, Jolts', in *The Journalist in the French Fin-de-Siècle: Enfants de la Presse* (Oxford: Legenda, 2018), 52–94

Rennie, Nicholas, 'Benjamin and Zola: Narrative, the Individual, and Crowds in an Age of Mass Production', *Comparative Literature Studies* 33: 4 (1996), 396–413

Robb, Graham, 'Madame Zola', in *Parisians: An Adventure History of Paris* (London: Picador, 2010), 175–97

Rosen, Michael, *The Disappearance of Emile Zola: Love, Literature and the Dreyfus Case* (London: Faber, 2017)

Samuels, Maurice, *Alfred Dreyfus: The Man at the Center of the Affair* (New Haven, CT: Yale University Press, 2024)

Schor, Naomi, 'Introduction', *Zola*, special issue, *Yale French Studies* 42 (1969), 5–7

Seillan, Jean-Marie, 'L'Afrique utopique de *Fécondité*', *Cahiers naturalistes* 75 (2001), 183–202

Trilling, Lionel, 'In Defense of Zola' (1953), in Trilling, *A Gathering of Fugitives* (London: Secker & Warburg, 1957), 12–19

Vizetelly, Ernest Alfred, *With Zola in England: A Story of Exile* (London: Chatto & Windus, 1898)

Wells, William D., 'Computer Simulation of Consumer Behavior', in Edward C. Bursk and John F. Chapman (eds.), *Modern Marketing Strategy* (1964; New York: New American Library, 1965), 104–14

White, Claire, *Work and Leisure in Late Nineteenth-Century French Culture* (London: Palgrave Macmillan, 2014)

White, Nicholas, *The Family in Crisis in Late Nineteenth-Century French Fiction* (Cambridge: Cambridge University Press, 1999)

Wilson, Angus, *Emile Zola: An Introductory Study of his Novels* (1952; 2nd ed. London: Secker & Warburg, 1964)

Woolf, Virginia, 'Professions for Women' (1931), in Rachel Bowlby (ed.), *The Crowded Dance of Modern Life* (London: Penguin, 1993), 101–6

Woollen, Geoff, 'Zola's Halles, a *Grande Surface* before Their Time', *Romance Studies* 18: 1 (June 2000), 21–30

Yee, Jennifer, 'Émile Zola's Black Lives: Colonial Experiments and the Limits of Empathy in *La Joie de vivre*', *Dix-Neuf* 28: 1 (2022), 1–15

Zola, Émile, *Carnets d'enquête: Une ethnographie inédite de la France*, ed. Henri Mitterand (Paris: France Loisirs, 1987)

Zola, Émile, *Lettres à Alexandrine 1876–1901*, eds. Brigitte Émile-Zola and Alain Pagès (Paris: Gallimard, 2014)

Zola, Émile, *Lettres à Jeanne Rozerot 1882–1902*, eds. Brigitte Émile-Zola and Alain Pagès (Paris: Gallimard, 2004)

Zola, Émile, *Les Manuscrits et les dessins de Zola: Notes préparatoires et dessins des 'Rougon-Macquart'*, eds. Olivier Lumbroso and Henri Mitterand, 3 vols. (Paris: Textuel, 2002)

Zola, Émile, *Mes haines* (1866), ed. François-Marie Mourad (Paris: Garnier Flammarion, 2012)

Zola, Émile, *Le Roman expérimental* (1880), ed. Aimé Guedj (Paris: Garnier Flammarion, 1971)

Zola, Émile, *Zola journaliste: Articles et chroniques*, ed. Adeline Wrona (Paris: Éditions Flammarion, 2011)

# INDEX

*Note to digital readers: page-spans may differ slightly from those listed below.*

*Absolutely Fabulous* 49, 139n2
adultery, literature of 45-6, 56, 91, 105, 138n46
AI 27
Aix-en-Provence 17, 31, 37
*An Officer and a Gentleman* 142n2
*An Officer and a Spy* 142n2
Anschluss (Nazi annexation of Austria) 126
antisemitism 83, 87, 126
　*see also* Dreyfus affair
Apelles 137n31
arcades 55-8, 139n8
Austen, Jane, *Pride and Prejudice* 53

bakeries 51
Balzac, Honoré de 6
Baudelaire, Charles, *Le Peintre de la vie moderne* (*The Painter of Modern Life*) 15
Bellamy, Edward, *Looking Backward* 20
Benjamin, Walter 56-7, 139-40n8
bicycling 86-7, 143n5
Bildungsroman 30, 60
birthrate, decline in 101, 105
Bloch-Dano, Evelyne, *Madame Zola* 89
*Blood, Sex and Money* 139n4
Bon Marché (department store) 10-11, 50
book marketing 26, 43, 146-7n48
boredom 95
Bowlby, Rachel 140n13, 146n42
breastfeeding 133, 145-6n42
Brooks, Peter 139n5
Burns, Colin 142-3n5

Catholicism 104
Céard, Henry 138n46
　*Une belle journée* 138n46
Cézanne, Paul 31, 140n22

Chatto & Windus 117
childlessness. 88-9, 101, 107-9, 144n27
class 8-9, 15-16, 20-2, 65, 106, 110-13, 145-6n42
colonialism 113
computers 27
consumer behaviour, modelling of 11-12, 27-8, 80-1
contraception 102-4, 108
Counter, Andrew 12, 145n28
course syllabuses 52
Crystal Palace 86

Darwin, Charles, *On the Origin of Species* 15, 50
department stores 48-50, 59-67, 77-8, 81
depopulation 105
Desmoulin, Fernand 100, 117-19, 125, 130-2, 148n52
Dickens, Charles, *Hard Times* 20
display x-xi, 58-60, 62-4
Dreyfus affair 83-7, 92-3, 95, 114-15, 132-3, 142n2, 142n3, 147n48
Dreyfus, Alfred xiv, 83, 95, 115, 142n2
Drouard, Alain 145n32
Duffy, Larry 145n29

electric-light advertising 146n48
Émile-Zola, Brigitte (Zola's great-granddaughter) 89-90
Émile-Zola, Denise (Zola's daughter) xiv, 85, 88-9, 109
Émile-Zola, Jacques (Zola's son) xiv, 85, 88-9, 109, 143n10
Enfants trouvés (charity) 89
Esterhazy, Ferdinand 85
eugenics 105-6

# INDEX

everyday life xi, 3, 14–15, 19–20, 48, 55, 68, 83–7, 90, 93–7, 130, 132–3
experimental novel 25–6, 30, 44, 90
  *see also* naturalism

fashion market 59, 63
Fasquelle, Eugène 95–6, 113
feminist history 49–50, 53
Ferrer, Daniel 141–2n35
*feuilleton* form 12, 98
flat characters 7–9, 11, 40, 81
  *see also* profile, types
Flaubert, Gustave x
  *Madame Bovary* 138n46
Fliess, Wilhelm 126
Forster, E.M. 7–9, 11
Fourier, Charles 139n8
Franco-Prussian war 16, 85
French Revolution 21–2
Freud, Sigmund 126–31, 137n30
  'Contribution to a Questionnaire on Reading' 127
  *The Interpretation of Dreams* 131
  'Observations on Transference Love' 128–30
  *Three Essays on the Theory of Sexuality* 104
  'Wolf Man' case 32

Gaskell, Elizabeth, *Mary Barton* 20
gender divisions, Zola's attention to 10, 42–3, 64–7
Girardin, Émile de, *Les Deux sœurs* 34–5
Goncourt, Edmond 144n27
  and Jules, *Germinie Lacerteux* 36

Hachette 26, 33
Harris, Robert, *An Officer and a Spy* 84, 142n2
Harris, Ruth 142n3
Harrow, Susan 137n31, 140n22
Harvey Nichols (department store) 49
Haussmann, Baron 1
Hemmings, F.W.J. ix
historical narrative 83–4, 86
Holmes, Oliver Wendell, Jr 125–6
Homer xi, 2, 12, 64, 127
*hypermarchés* 51

incest 38–9, 138n40

industrial novel 20, 52, 60–1
infertility 111
Institute of Journalists 88
interiors, representation of 45–6

*J'Accuse* (film) 142n2
  *see also* Zola, Works, *J'Accuse!*
James, Henry 143n7
Jameson, Fredric x–xi
journalism 11, 33, 87–8, 137n32, 143n6

Kafka, Franz, 'The Metamorphosis' 120–1
Keating, Peter 147n48
Kelly, Jill 144n25
Kipling, Rudyard, *The Jungle Book* 127

Labori, Fernand 132
labour history 49, 52–3, 60–1
Lapière, Marie 147n48
Leeds 49
Lethbridge, Robert 140n22
letter-writing 86–8, 115–16
Ligue pour la Régénération humaine 105–6
Lip watchmaking co-operative 147n48
loss leaders 62–3
Louvre (department store) 11
Lumley, Joanna 139n2

Macaulay, Thomas Babington 127
*magasins de nouveautés* 58–9
Malthus, Thomas 105–6
markets 16, 51, 141n33
Médan 101, 118, 144n27
menopause, literary representation of 41
milieux xiii, 8, 12, 25, 27–8, 47, 69–70, 84, 90, 106, 138n1
Miller, Michael B., *The Bon Marché* 50
Milton, John, *Paradise Lost* 127
Mitterand, Henri 146n48
Moineaud (Zolas' cat) 148n50
Monnier, Pauline 116–17
Morris, William, *News from Nowhere* 20
Musset, Alfred de, *Le Caprice* 45

naturalism 33, 36
  *see also* experimental novel
Nicholas, Brian, 47, 138n1
Niger Convention, 1898 113
Noiray, Jacques 147n48

# INDEX

*Nottingham French Studies* 142n5

omniscient narrator 10, 14–15, 43
online shopping 50–1

Pagès, Alain 90, 144n18, 147n50
paradise 79, 113, 132–3
*The Paradise* (TV serial) 53, 139n4
*Il paradiso delle signore* (TV serial) 53, 139n4
parenthood 87–9, 100–13
Paris Commune 16
Péguy, Charles 112–13
pets 147n50
photography 98–100, 144n25
Picquart, Georges 85, 116–17, 142n2
Pin (Zolas' dog) 147n50
Pliny the Elder 137n31
Polanski, Roman, *An Officer and a Spy* 84, 142n2
poster advertising 18, 114, 133, 146n48
primal scene 32
profile xiii, 1–46, 80–2
   in art 4–5
   in digital culture 6–7
   in Christian iconography 5–6
   *see also* flat characters, types

Queen's Hotel, Upper Norwood 86, 94

race 9, 106, 137–8n39
realism 6, 10, 52–3, 90
Rees, Kate 137n32
Renan, Ernest, *Vie de Jésus* (*The Life of Jesus*) 5–6
Rennie, Nicholas 140n8
reproductive politics 101–13
retail history 49–52
Richardson, Samuel, *Pamela* 53
Rifkin, Adrian 140n8
Robb, 143n9
Rosen, Michael 142n3
Rougon-Macquart novel cycle xiii, 8, 16–17, 44, 47, 55, 61, 126–7, 138n40, 139n4, 141–2n35, 143n7
Rozerot, Jeanne xiv, 85, 91, 98–9, 143n10

Samuels, Maurice 142n3
Saunders, Jennifer 139n2
Schopenhauer, Arthur 9, 105

Schor, Naomi ix
science and literature 26–8, 90–1
Second Empire 16, 61
Seillan, Jean-Marie 137–8n39
serialization 12, 98, 114, 139n4
sexual harrassment 66
sexuality 54, 103–4, 108, 110–12
Shakespeare, William 127
shops and shopping xiii–xiv, 47–82, 86–7
shop windows 55–60, 62–4
   *see also* window-shopping
silhouette 4–5
sitcoms 49, 139n2
soap operas 53
social history 84, 90
souvenirs 99, 140–1n22
Spalding, Annette 116–17
Spalding, Percy 116–17
stereotypes 9
Surrey 86–7, 99
surrogacy 145–6n42
supermarkets 51
symbolism 105
*la symphonie des fromages* x–xi

translations of Zola's novels 86, 98, 147n48
Trilling, Lionel vii–viii
Twain, Mark, *Sketches* 127
types 6, 13, 78, 91
   *see also* flat characters, profiles, stereotypes

Upper Norwood 86, 99, 141n22
   *see also* Zola, exile in England

Vizetelly, Ernest 86–7, 117, 143n6, 147n48
Vizetelly, Henry 147n48

Wagner, Richard 105
wet-nursing 111, 145–6n42
Weybridge 86
White, Claire 144n23
White, Nicholas 138n40
Williams, Rowan 5
Wilson, Angus vii–ix
window-shopping 99, 141n22
   *see also* shop windows
Wood, Michael ix

# INDEX

Woolf, Virginia, 'Professions for Women' 97–8
Woollen, Geoff 141n33

*Yale French Studies* ix
Yee, Jennifer 138n39

Zola, Alexandrine xiv, 84, 91, 98–9, 108–9, 113–18, 134, 140–1n2, 143n10, 147–8n50
Zola, Émile
  early life 30–1, 37, 91
  exile in England 86–7, 91–2, 95–100, 132–4, 141n22, 142–3n5
  working practice 10–11, 32–5, 37, 43–4, 82, 93–8, 132–3, 136n20, 144n26
  Works
  L'Amour des bêtes' ('The Love of Animals') 147n50
  *L'Argent* (*Money*) xii, 16
  'L'Argent dans la littérature' ('Money in Literature') 34
  *L'Assommoir* (*The Assommoir*) xii, 68–76, 78–81, 118
  *La Bête humaine* 17
  *Au Bonheur des Dames* (*The Ladies' Paradise*) x–xi, 1–4, 10–14, 17, 48–54, 59–69, 78–9, 120, 139n8
  'J'accuse' 85–6, 142n2
  'Causerie du dimanche' 18
  *La Confession de Claude* 26, 28–32, 34, 37–9, 91
  *La Conquête de Plassans* (*The Conquest of Plassans*) 119–25
  *Contes à Ninon* 26
  *La Curée* (*The Kill*) 16, 79
  *La Débâcle* (*The Débâcle*) xii, 16
  'Dépopulation' 91, 105
  *Le Docteur Pascal* 127, 138n40
  'L'Encre et le sang' 88
  *La Faute de l'Abbé Mouret* (*The Sin of Abbé Mouret*) xii
  *Fécondité* xiv, 92, 100–15, 132–3, 139n8, 144n26, 146–7n48, 147n50
  *La Fortune des Rougon* (*The Fortune of the Rougons*) xii, 17
  *Germinal* 16, 18–22, 52, 73
  'Germinie Lacerteux' 36–7
  *J'accuse!* 85–6, 142n2
  *La Joie de vivre* (*The Bright Side of Life*) 8–9, 68
  'Lettre à la jeunesse' ('Letter to Young People') 5
  *Lettres à Alexandrine* 83–5, 113–17
  *Lettres à Jeanne Rozerot* 85, 91, 97
  *Lourdes* 17, 104, 147n48
  *Madeleine Férat* 26, 38–44, 91
  *Nana* 54
  *L'Œuvre* 31, 78
  *Pages d'exil* 86, 142–3n50
  *Paris* 17, 143n5, 147n48
  *Pot-Bouille* (*Pot Luck*) xii, 16, 120
  *Le Roman expérimental* (*The Experimental Novel*) 25
  *Rome* 17, 104, 147n48
  'Le Supplice d'une femme et Les Deux Sœurs' 34–5
  *La Terre* (*The Earth*) 147n48
  *Thérèse Raquin* 22–6, 38–41, 43, 55–9, 63, 67, 69, 91, 139n8
  *Travail* (*Work*) 20, 133, 144n23, 146–7n48
  *Une page d'amour* (*A Love Story*) 17–18, 44–6, 137n46
  *Le Ventre de Paris* (*The Belly of Paris*) x, 16, 68, 76–80
  *Vérité* (*Truth*) 147n48
Zola, Émilie (Zola's mother) 31, 91
Zola, François (Zola's father) 31, 91